GW00786459

Mayfair Madams

Mayfair Madams

Maria Perry

Illustrations by
Bernard Cookson

ANDRE DEUTSCH

First published in Great Britain in1999 by
André Deutsch Limited
76 Dean Street
London
WIV 5HA
www.vci.co.uk

A catalogue record for this book is available from the British Library

ISBN 0 233 99476 9

Typeset by Derek Doyle & Associates
Mold, Flintshire
Printed in the UK by MPG Books,
Bodmin, Cornwall.

For Zeta

Contents

1. Mayfair 1
2. Noise 8
3. His First Duchess 15
4. The Flat That Never Was 19
5. Till Debts Us Do Part 22
6. Dangerous to Know 27
7. Little America 32
8. 'A Nightingale Sang' 40
9. Heirs and Graces 50
10. French Lessons 57
11. Money 66
12. Shopping to Survive 77
13. Marriage in Mayfair 87
14. Charity Begins in Mayfair 94
15. Flora and Fauna 102
16. Shopping to Impress 111

Acknowledgements

My thanks are due to the Royal Literary Fund and Mr Philip Lawton, QC for enabling me to rest between serious works to research this *jeu d'esprit.*

1
Mayfair

Histories of Mayfair will tell you that a May Fair of great size and notoriety was held annually in a buttercup meadow near Hyde Park. It began when James II granted letters patent for a fourteen-day cattle market to take place from the first of May. There was much merry-making. Country folk came to London with fat cows for sale, and the Londoners streamed out of their smoky city to get a breath of fresh air, for the sea coal fires which our ancestors used to heat their homes, created almost as much pollution in Westminster then as there is now.

In the fields that bordered the River Tyburn the Londoners disported themselves like nymphs and shepherds at a rite of spring. The young gambolled round a maypole. Booths and tents dispensed cakes and ale. Jugglers, strolling players, sausage sellers and dancing bears trampled the daisies. Pedlars did a roaring trade in ribbons and hat trims. The revels lasted all night long, attracting thieves, pickpockets and drunks. There was also a good deal of wenching.

Naturally, therefore, the story of Mayfair revolves around its womenfolk. Heiresses, duchesses, dancers and show-girls with now and then a liberal sprinkling of royal mistresses, they were rabid consumers of luxury goods. Some were tarts, some *grande dames* of high renown. Their housing requirements were uniformly palatial, and happily their needs coincided with the building boom in Georgian London. Arbiters of fashion through the ages, such ladies brought trade and quality to a district that thrives upon both.

Bounded nowadays by Park Lane, Piccadilly, Regent Street and Oxford Street, Mayfair is the most clearly defined of London's villages. It is a place where money flows fast and where property changes hands with the speed of counters on a Monopoly board. Its residents have a fierce sense of corporate identity. By night it is a playground for the rich, its clubs and restaurants exuding an aura of discreet wealth. By day it is a centre of international banking, art sales, oil deals and *haute* commerce. Its shoe shops are patronised by the most extravagant women in the world. Its hairdressers are packed drier-to-basin with faces which smile monthly from the covers of *Vogue*. The story that Nicky Clarke charges £250 for a haircut is not a myth, and a used car sprayed a tasteful shade of foxglove, purchased from a Park Lane dealer, can set the buyer back a casual £50,000. Over the years Mayfair has been the scene of more glittering parties and society scandals than any other square mile on the Earth's crust. Its policemen are the most laid-back in our land, its parking wardens have hearts as hard as industrial diamonds and its call girls belong to off-shore tax syndicates.

But to return to the May Fair. Queen Anne loathed the noise. It was horrible when, as Princess, she lived in rented accommodation in Piccadilly. Later it disturbed her royal slumber when, as Queen of England, she was half a mile away at St James's Palace. As heiress to the throne, Anne had quarrelled with her childless sister, Queen Mary, who reigned jointly with her husband William. The royal couple lived more than a mile away from London at Kensington Palace, where the air was healthier and eased the King's asthma. The Princess, whose taste was more regal than that of the Queen, rented Berkeley House, an imposing pile which stood on the site now bounded by Berkeley Street and Stratton Street. It had been built by Lord Berkeley of Stratton, Lord Lieutenant of Ireland in the reign of Charles II, and its extensive grounds were eventually to form Berkeley Square. Lord Berkeley died in 1678. His widow, Lady Berkeley, was one of Mayfair's earliest and shrewdest developers. The daughter of Sir Andrew Riccard, Governor of the East India Company, she had inherited her father's talent for business. She let out some of her extensive gardens as building lands, netting astronomical ground rents of almost £1,000 a year, which led John Evelyn, the diarist to comment on 'the mad intemperance of the age'. The leases brought in huge profits to the Berkeley family for the next 200 years and Lady Berkeley added to her increments by letting the house to Princess Anne at a rent of £600 a year.

Having clinched the deal, the old dowager was very slow to move out of the premises and drove the Princess nearly frantic with her prevarications. Berkeley House had a scented staircase of cedarwood and a prodigious number of rooms. On first visiting it Anne offended Lady Berkeley by not inspecting every single attic. To hasten the Berkeleys' departure she offered them accommodation in the Cockpit, a house in the precincts of the Palace of Whitehall, which Queen Mary had rather grudgingly allowed her sister to use when she married the lacklustre Prince George of Denmark. In 1692, when the dowager finally vacated her house, the Princess moved there with an enormous household and her friends John and Sarah Churchill, who had been the cause of her quarrel with the Queen. Amidst general grumblings about Civil List payments, Anne rented two extra houses for her retinue. As the royal tiff was public knowledge, most courtiers declined to visit the Princess. It was not until Mary's death that the value of land in Piccadilly soared because the heiress to the throne was a resident of Mayfair.

When Mary died, William patched up relations with his sister-in-law. The courtiers flocked to Berkeley House, with only Evelyn, a latent conservationist, complaining about the 'vandalism' which had begun with Lady Berkeley carving up her gardens. William assigned a wing of St James's Palace to Anne and Prince George, but during the three years she lived in Piccadilly the future Queen took a lasting dislike to the May Fair. In the final months of Anne's stay, a bold thief slipped into Berkeley House and casually helped himself to a solid silver cistern. This hot item was sold to a distiller in Twickenham and set the pattern for a long tradition of stealing *objets de vertu* from the British aristocracy. Together with the dreadful racket that assaulted her ears every May, floating across from Shepherd Market and in through her back windows, the theft set the seal on Anne's disapproval. One of her first acts on coming to the throne was to attempt to suppress the Fair her father had founded.

James II's grant for the cattle market, however, had been made in perpetuity, and only an Act of Parliament could abolish it. This painful knowledge must have taken an extra toll on Queen Anne's nerves, while they were measuring her up for her coronation robes. She had not yet hit the brandy bottle, but she was already getting an inkling that life as a constitutional monarch might not be all cakes and ale. She contented herself with a royal writ to restrain undesirable persons from attending the May Fair.

Medical historians may disagree, but I imagine Queen Anne had been in culture shock ever since moving from Syon House near Brentford. There, the Thames flowed softly and the sheep grazed safely in a park whose eco-systems had not yet been disturbed by Capability Brown and his cohorts of ambitious gardeners. At Syon cattle waiting to have their portraits painted by Albert Cuyp, the Dutch cow painter, lay peacefully chewing the cud, and bird song wafted through the casements. Presumably Queen Anne, as Princess, had confidently thrown open those back windows of hers in Piccadilly in anticipation of listening to nightingales trilling away in Berkeley Square. It was a nasty surprise therefore, on the evening of 1 May 1693, on returning from taking the waters at Bath as a cure for her dreadful gout, that the heiress to the throne heard rioting and drunkenness floating across the London air instead of sweet chirruping.

Knowing that his brother James was a Roman Catholic, Anne's uncle, King Charles II, had taken good care to have his nieces instructed in the Anglican faith – an obligatory requirement for future queens. As a confirmed member of the Church of England Anne knew that once rioting and drunkeness is proven, chambering and wantoness cannot be far behind. Uncle Charles himself had been a case in point. She made it clear that a clean-up of court morals was on the agenda, but it was a harder task to impress her views on the Londoners.

In 1701, the last year of William's reign, an up-market crowd had attended the May Fair. Brian Fairfax wrote to a friend, 'All the nobility in Town were there.' He went on rapturously to praise 'the beauty, shape and activity' of Lady Mary who, when she danced, entranced his cousin, Lord Fairfax, and many other young noblemen who mingled with the citizens. Brian Fairfax had been equerry to Charles II and King William. He was something of a connoisseur and greatly admired a detailed architectural model of the City of Amsterdam, ten yards in diameter with 'every street, every individual house' carved in wood 'in exact proportion', which was being displayed at one of the stalls. Craft fairs were clearly under way and the whole thing sounds a far cry from the drunken rabble of which Queen Anne had complained.

By 1702, however, things had obviously declined. There was a near riot when three girls were mistakenly arrested as prostitutes. A constable was run through with a rapier by Thomas Cook, a gallant butcher, who had tried to protect the girls. He was hanged at Tyburn, while the dead constable was given a hero's funeral at St James's Church, Piccadilly. High Anglican, of course, and it was very much hoped that the accompanying sermon and the constable's coffin, tastefully framed by all that Grinling Gibbons carving behind the altar, would arouse public sympathy. However, the Fair was not suppressed, but merely frowned upon, and the following year the noise from the nocturnal revels went on as loud as ever.

Not long afterwards those omnipotent kill-joys the Westminster Magistrates got in on the act. They declared the May Fair 'a tumultuous assembly' which encouraged 'loose, idle and disorderly persons' to 'allure young persons and servants to meet, game and to commit lewd and disorderly practices.' Queen Anne, swift to spot an opportunity for noise abatement and still straining her ears to catch up with the sweet notes of the elusive nightingale, chimed in with a Royal Proclamation. It forbade the erection of booths, stalls or side-shows, and for the rest of her reign the May Fair was restricted to the selling of cows. Cuyp had died in the Netherlands and representational art has never seen his like since, so the bovine beauties didn't get to be hung in the Tate or the National Gallery.

Lamenting the decline of the May Fair in 1709 *Tatler* published a snide state of the arts piece, pointing out that the scene had now moved to Greenwich, where Mr Penkethman, a popular impressario, had set up his company of strolling players. The menagerie, which had been a regular feature of the Fair, was up for auction and *Tatler* ingenuously hinted that if any lady or gentleman had occasion to purchase a tame elephant Mr Penkethman could oblige. If George of Denmark sat up in bed sipping his chocolate that morning and scanning *Tatler*, while his valet powdered his wig, I hope he detected the undertone of swingeing rebuke. So nice to think of the early glossies sounding the clarion call for actors' salaries.

Meanwhile, Queen Anne's old landlady, Lady Berkeley, had created legal havoc with her leases. As soon as it was learned that King William intended to move Anne from Berkeley House to St James's Palace, the news had spread about London like wildfire that the old lady would be selling up. The Duke of Devonshire and the Marquis of Normanby (later Duke of Buckingham) both made bids, but it was never clear which of them had first option, though it soon appeared that Lady Berkeley had sold her property twice over. The case was referred to Chancery, where it emerged that Devonshire had paid a £500 deposit. By the spring of 1695 he moved into Berkeley House, which was re-named Devonshire House. The Chancery case dragged on for another two years and even though the Duke had paid £11,000 to Lady Berkeley's son for the freehold, it was not until December 1697 that the Lord Chancellor and the Lord Chief Justice jointly dismissed Normanby's claim. The Duke, who spent most of his time at Chatsworth anyway, had previously, when in London, rented a charming country villa south east of Hyde Park Corner from the Duchess of Grafton. It was called Arlington House. When Devonshire's lease expired, Normanby bought the property and upon becoming a Duke himself, re-built what was eventually to be known as Buckingham Palace.

In the meantime the Duke of Devonshire, irritated by the length of the proceedings in Chancery, had a fair premonition that Piccadilly was due to become a built-up area. He drafted some tricky legal jargon to prevent Lord Berkeley's heirs from developing bits of Berkeley Square in a manner which might spoil his view. The businesslike Lady Berkeley it must be remembered, had not *sold* her gardens, she had merely leased them. A clause forbidding the builders of Berkeley Square to annoy the Duke was accordingly slipped in. Sixty years later it was to prove a huge challenge to Robert Adam, commissioned by the

Marquis of Bute to build a house in the south-east corner of the square.

Despite Queen Anne's disapproval the May Fair sprang irreverently to life again as soon as George I was on the throne. Pedlars, jugglers, acrobats and fire-eaters swarmed back to Brook Field, the meadow upon which the cattle market took place. Prominent among the street vendors was Tiddy Dol, the gingerbread seller. Known as 'the King of itinerant tradesmen', he was a giant of a man and a popular figure at the May Fair, where he dressed in white silk stockings, a suit of white gold lace, with a lace-ruffled shirt and a hat smothered in feathers. He was immortalised by Hogarth in the picture of the 'Idle Prentice' going to execution and he had a curious repertoire of doggerel verse, which helped to sell his wares.

> *A wiscum, a riscum and a why not walk in?*
> *Here is your nice gingerbread, your spice gingerbread*
> *It will melt in your mouth like a red-hot brickbat*
> *And rumble inside you like Punch and his wheelbarrow*

he would intone, ending with a chorus of,

> *Tid-dy ti tid-dy tee*
> *Tid-dy ti-dy dol*

sung to the tune of a popular ballad. He is comemmorated lavishly at Tiddy Dol's Eating House, a restaurant beloved by American tourists on the corner of Hertford Street and Shepherd Market. The menu boasts 'English food with a French touch', which has been true of most English food since the Norman Conquest. Roly-poly pudding, spotted dick, fish and chips and an ancient gingerbread pudding featuring cinnamon and black treacle are all available, even on hot summer evenings, when the palate craves salads and sorbet.

Towards the end of the eighteenth century the Fair declined, but Mayfair retained the name and *Tatler* and the partying survive.

2
Noise

The battle against noise is on-going. In Shepherd Market, that tiny but expensive slice of real estate behind Curzon Street, there are four pubs, six restaurants with outside tables, nine pavement cafés, a private shebeen, a Polish–Mexican bistro and London's most controversial nightclub, Iceni. It follows that on a summers night, when the natives wish to throw open their casements to admit soft breezes, the clashing of cutlery, the clatter of crockery and the conversations of a hundred people dining alfresco combine into a thunderous cacophony. When the pubs close roisterers spill on to the narrow streets, adding to the raucous din. O'Neill's, the popular Irish tavern, flings wide its doors and wild bursts of Hibernian music rob the residents of their beauty sleep.

Just as the weary householders bury their heads in their pillows for the third time, a group of rich young revellers arrive at Iceni. Some are on motorbikes. Others, lured by the promise of 'valet parking', roar up the narrow alleyways in high-powered sports cars. Iceni is said to be completely sound-proofed, but the residents of Shepherd Market do not agree. The Rich Young Things who pay £500 a year for membership are obliged to form an orderly queue to get in, for Iceni is highly fashionable and patronised by the likes of Michael Jackson, the artist formerly known as Prince and Sylvester Stallone. Sometime between 2 and 4 am, when the good people of Shepherd Market have fallen into fitful slumber, the DJ politely asks the Rich Young Things to leave Iceni, because of the City of Westminster's licensing laws. *En masse* they pour into the streets, talking in unsubdued voices because they have had a good time. Occasionally the club's licence is withdrawn, but an appeal is immediately lodged with Westminster City Council at the Horseferry Road Magistrates' Court. By English law, while an appeal is in progress, premises may continue to operate. War has been waged between the proprietors of Iceni and the Mayfair Residents' Association for six years, but at the time of writing the club continues to flourish.

Among the residents this is a cause for tearing of hair and gnashing of teeth. Surprisingly, however, it has brought about a truce between two sets of deadly opponents, for Mayfair being a Very Superior Place, has two Very Superior Residents' Associations. Known locally as ARM and RAM, they hold rival garden parties, vie for coverage in the pages of the *Evening Standard*, spread slanderous gossip about each other and in general hate each other's guts. The War of the Iceni has united them against a common enemy and this year the *Mayfair Times* even celebrated the alliance by publishing pictures of the two garden parties on adjacent social pages.

On the right-hand side are pictures of Baroness Stephania von Kories Zu Goetzen looking best-dressed and Raine, Countess Spencer, who is, of course, the daughter of Barbara Cartland and sometime stepmother of the late Diana, Princess of Wales. Raine smiles graciously from under a coiffure of this season's 'Big Hair'. She goes to Josef, Mayfair's most prestigious hairdresser. He has no royal appointments, but everyone knows that he often washes royal hair. Josef is Mayfair's top tiara-fixer. On the morning of the State Opening of Parliament his staff go into overdrive. 'In the old days', he remembers, 'people didn't fuss so about tiaras. They would pop in in the early morning, have them fixed and put a headscarf over them, but now we need a whole team.' On the right-hand page of the *Mayfair Times*, Marilyn Luscombe, an erstwhile bodybuilder, now Director of the Association of Personal Trainers, seems bent on draping her commendable biceps in diamonds, as she tries out the free jewellery cleaning service, which was such a feature of the ARM party.

RAM stands for The Residents' Association of Mayfair and is the older and more official of the two. It was founded twenty-two years ago, when St Mark's Church of England nursery school was threatened with closure. Sundry parents united to save the treasured amenity. In Mayfair it is not so much a question of 'Love thy neighbour', as 'Who's thy neighbour?' In this case Linda and Geoffrey Howard, who had children at the school, rang Mrs Rowlandson (widow of the late Tiny) and a protest group was immediately mooted. Brigadier Viner, who had been Chairman of the Conservative Party, canvassed the area. Two hundred residents immediately pledged their support and elected the Brigadier Chairman. By common consent, Margaret, Duchess of Argyll, became Vice Chairman. The Duchess, who had been described by a divorce judge as the most sexually depraved woman in the land, might have seemed an unlikely champion for a C of E crèche devoted to the moral welfare of top tots, but the Conservative Party is strong in Mayfair and *esprit de classe* won the day.

While RAM is devoted to the ideal of keeping Mayfair residential, the aims of ARM are a little more commercial. It has been said – but please dear Reader, it has not been said by me, I only quote – that while the members of RAM have 'pull', the members of ARM are a tiny bit inclined to 'push'. ARM stands for Association of Residents of Mayfair. It is a breakaway group and its chairman, Richard Rawlinson, stood as a candidate for the Liberal Democrats, so, obviously, it is his duty to encourage change.

The main change Richard Rawlinson would like to see in Shepherd Market is the extinction of Iceni. The name derives from the ancient but conspicuously wealthy British tribe, based loosely in Norfolk and Suffolk. This tribe disagreed with the Roman authorities on the subject of tax collection and between 59 AD and 61 AD, they revolted, sacking London and St Albans in the process. Their Queen Boadicea – Boudicca in the vernacular – had been publicly whipped and her daughters raped. Not unnaturally, she sought revenge and dashed up from Norfolk in a nasty-looking chariot with knives on the wheels. There is a lively representation of Queen Boudicca in battle array on the corner of Westminster Bridge. She was defeated near Coventry and committed suicide. She is very beautifully commemorated in Lady Antonia Fraser's book, *Warrior Queens*, and also in the Iceni night club's little advertising pamphlet. This is tastefully bound in red plush and has a nice silver logo for Smirnoff vodka on the back. Queen Boudicca is mentioned in the Introduction, and local legend has it that the spot where she committed suicide was White Horse Street, where the club is currently located. A rival theory advanced by Sir Clive Sinclair, formerly Chairman of the Shepherd Market Association, is that she is buried under one of the platforms of King's Cross station.

I do not know if Mr Rawlinson has ever been inside the Iceni. If so he probably wouldn't find much to complain about. The murals aren't a patch on anything in Old Pompeii. Anyone hoping for an erotic thrill would be much better advised to study the Cranach nymphs in the National Gallery. On the ground floor of the nightclub, there is a room where the very young dance under ultraviolet lighting. A tribal area on the second floor plays some of the best Euro-disco in town. The sofas are covered in politically correct fake tiger skin and hunting trophies which would not disgrace the Carlton or the Reform clubs hang on the walls – except, of course, they are made of fibreglass. The popular myth that the top floor is a harem where rich orientals disport themselves like Roman Emperors on campaign is untrue. There are tables and chairs and a bar, which serves Dom Perignon and Cristalle Roederer. Eastern gentlemen do drink there in the company of pretty girls, but the same may be said of the Grosvenor House Hotel and the Dorchester. The nearest thing to a Roman orgy that ever happened at Iceni was when Sylvester Stallone arrived and said 'Bring me girls'. The place was crawling with teeny-bopper autograph hunters, so the properietors complied. Stallone retired with writer's cramp.

This is not to say that anyone living within a quarter mile radius of White Horse Street does not have a valid grudge. The proprietors of Iceni would be the first to admit that two hundred of the Rich Young Things all ejected into the street at closing time can make a helluva din, but not even those practised vigilantes the Westminster Noise Team can do much about it. There is, after all, no law against talking at 2 am, even when it *is* under someone else's windows. The City of Westminster runs a crack little unit of Noise Officers. There are sixteen to twenty permanent staff, a minimum of four on duty on any given day. If the public ring to complain of anything from builders' drills to rogue burglar alarms, an Environmental Health Officer with thousands of pounds worth of equipment for measuring decibels will be round like a shot. Or at any rate as fast as the traffic permits. The trouble is sometimes the traffic doesn't permit, so there are certain faults inherent in the system. In Shepherd Market these worked in favour of the Romanian gypsies.

Adding to all the noise emanating from the restaurants and pavement cafés, one summer there arrived a group of itinerant Central European buskers. Mrs Marreco, the wife of Tony Marreco, the President of RAM, insists they were Romanian. The problem was that they never stayed anywhere long enough for anyone to ascertain the true facts. Mr Marreco is rather good on facts. He is a retired barrister who has lived in Shepherd Market for fifty-three years. He co-founded Amnesty International and after the Second World War he was Junior Counsel at the Nuremburg Trials. A man of the law, you might say. His biggest asset in Shepherd Market is Mrs Marreco, who is beautiful and Brazilian and filled with the sort of inner radiance which makes people feel better just to say 'Good Morning' to her. She is a brilliant cook, a superb hostess, a talented interior decorator and universally beloved in Shepherd Market, as the best-mannered patron of everyone from the chemist to the fishmonger.

Mrs Marreco is also a gardener of distinction. When she and Mr Marreco lived at Port Hall in Co. Donegal, which rates several pages in one of Desmond Guinness's *Irish Country House* books, she created one of the finest gardens in Europe, which covered an area roughly the size of the whole of Shepherd Market. When visitors from the American chapter of the Irish Georgian Society came to admire the architectural proportions of Port Hall, and the dining room with its hand-painted wallpaper, they would exclaim with delight at Mrs Marreco's garden, embellished as it was in its heyday, by two live peacocks called Denis and Margaret. Nowadays Mrs Marreco tunes in to all the TV gardening programmes, occasionally exhibiting a faint curl of the lip at the bit when the presenter empties out the ubiquitous gravel round the pampas grass and discourses rapturously about *iris pseudacorus*.* *Iris pseudacorus* grows wild in Ireland.

* Yellow flags.

12

*Mrs Marreco seized her plant spray, took aim and misfired, drenching
the diners outside L'Artiste Musclé.*

It came about that Mrs Marreco – who has just run up a couple of enchanting little terraces in Wiltshire with fruit trees, two ponds and a profusion of hardy perennials – was tending her scented geraniums one evening in Shepherd Market, when the Romanian buskers appeared out of nowhere and began to serenade the public at large. 'They shake their tambourines and twang a double bass,' she recalls. Mrs M promptly rang the Westminster Noise number. The yuppies outside the Grapes had been whooping it up for hours, you understand. O'Neill's was in full swing with the doors wide open and a selection, which ranged from the 'Londonderry Air' to the Chieftains was floating outwards and upwards. Cutlery clashing and crockery rattling were going full blast outside the Sofra and Al-Hamra restaurants, so that the double bass twanging rhythmically above all was the last straw. Playfully Mrs M threatened the Romanians with her plant spray. Thinking it great fun they smiled and waved, redoubling their efforts to please the beautiful lady peeping out above her pretty window boxes. In due course the Westminster Noise Team arrived, but by this time the Romanians had circled the square, collected from the gourmets outside Le Boudin Blanc, fleeced an American Jewish couple outside Tiddy Dols for a few bars of 'Hava Nagila' and vanished up Curzon Street.

As soon as the Noise officers left, the Romanians came back. It was about half-past ten and they wanted to say 'Good Night' to the nice lady with the geraniums. The Westminster Noise number was engaged. Mrs Marreco paced the carpet for some minutes before taking action. The twanging increased and the tambourines were shaken with Bacchanalian vigour. Mrs Marreco seized her plant spray, took aim and mis-fired, drenching the diners outside L'Artiste Muscle. The episode has left her with a great distaste for summer nights in the Metropolis. 'Nowadays,' she says, 'I only like London when it's raining.'

3
His First Duchess

If we had followed the progress of the Romanian gypsies, as they fled from the Noise Inspectors, we would have come to the Al-Hamra Restaurant in Shepherd Street. Here a blue plaque proclaims the exact site of the May Fair. Across the way, in tasteful gold lettering on a claret-coloured ground, the Shepherd Tavern volunteers the information that the Market is named after its developer, Edward Shepherd, the architect, who in 1735 obtained a grant from George II to build on Brook Field. The first permanent structure to replace the old booths was a two-storey dwelling with a butcher's shop below and a Great Room above, which doubled as a theatre in May Week. A few yards away, up the cobbled alley known as Market Mews, a brand new dark green plaque offers a more pastoral theory. The plaque is set in the arch which leads into the mews from Hertford Street. It announces, 'On this site stood Mayfair's oldest house, the Cottage 1618 AD from where a shepherd tended his flock, while Tyburn idled nearby.'

Linguistic purists enjoy pointing out that if the Market had been named after the sheep farmer, there would be an apostrophe after Shepherd, which there is not. The green plaque, however, regularly enchants patrons of the Hilton Mews Hotel, which has been done up in Thameside red brick with a *rus in urbe* interior, so all parties are kept happy. The Hilton Mews has gone in for particularly luxuriant hanging baskets in recent years, which must delight clients of the 'Fresh young models', who practise on the opposite side of the street under charmingly old-fashioned red light bulbs. As they enter the Georgian doorways to sin expensively behind lace curtains, the customers no doubt sniff the flowers and fancy themselves bound for

Elysium. In these times of dizzying social change, it must be comforting for them to see figure modelling advertised in the time-honoured way. Soho nowadays has become so blatant, with the word MODEL luridly displayed on orange neon signs.

Ten years before Shepherd developed his market, Sir Richard Grosvenor began to lay out Mayfair's grandest square on the estate he inherited from his parents, Sir Thomas Grosvenor, a Cheshire baronet and Mary Davies, the 13-year-old child bride who brought over 100 acres of fine agricultural land into the family. The desirable heiress had been wooed since she was eight years old, for as well as owning the fields south of Oxford Street and east of Tyburn she had been left a vast fortune by her millionaire relation, Hugh Audley, Clerk to the Court of Wards and moneylender to the nobility. It followed that Sir Richard was not short of funds. He is often credited with being Mayfair's premier builder, but as a developer he was pipped to the post by the businesslike Lady Berkeley. You will remember she had leased off strips of her garden at rents which robbed John Evelyn of his breath and then lured royalty to the area. Now, according to the *Oxford English Dictionary* 'Madam', besides being a title of respect, means 'a lady of rank; a minx; a hussy; a brothel-keeper, or a sharp-witted female person'. Shrewd old Lady Berkeley certainly fell into the last category. The rents from Berkeley Square began to rise steadily from the moment Queen Anne came to the throne and they have continued to do so, annually, for the last three hundred years.

Sir Richard Grosvenor meanwhile, aspired to upward mobility. As the son of a Cheshire baronet, he became MP for Chester like his father before him. Very *old* blood coursed through his veins. The name Grosvenor derives from respectable Norman French, 'Gros Veneur' meaning Fat Hunter, but on his mother's side Sir Richard had inherited disgracefully *new* money. Naturally, therefore, he wished to consolidate his position in Society by attracting the Quality to his square. As luck would have it George I's mistress, the Duchess of Kendal, had moved out of St James's Palace and was house-hunting. She took a fancy to No 43 and became the square's first duchess. Although she outlived the King by sixteen years, she must have reflected on past glories each time she opened her front door. When planning his square, the young baronet from the north had loyally placed an equestrian statue of the reigning monarch as its centrepiece. This enabled the Duchess to gaze fondly at the tubby figure of her lover, dressed as a Roman Emperor and gilded from head to toe.

After George I died, the Duchess retained No 43, but spent more time at her villa in Isleworth. According to Horace Walpole, when a raven flew through her window, she was persuaded it was the soul of the late King. In a moment of Teutonic sentimentality, he had assured her they would not even be parted by death. In life he was a despicable old two-timer, which can't have done much for his image in the American colonies, with their profound regard for moral decency. The English took a more tolerant view – better a man with two mistresses than a Roman Catholic on the throne. Since Baroness Kielmansegge, later Countess of Darlington was short and fat, and the Duchess tall and skinny, Londoners immediately nicknamed the pair 'the Elephant' and 'the Maypole'. Both ladies made vast fortunes in 1720 out of the South Sea Bubble. Hogarth portrayed the investors in this incredible speculation riding high on a merry-go-round which led to nowhere. Four hundred and sixty-two MPs held stock and, when the bubble burst, the Chancellor of the Exchequer was expelled from the House of Commons and committed to the Tower. While imprisoned there, he invested the remainder of his fortune in a house in Grosvenor Square.

Despite her English title, the Duchess was a von Schulenburg, whose thoughtless parents had christened her Ehrengard Melusina. She was an avid collector of titles and as Duchess of Munster developed an interest in Anglo–Irish credit transactions. Shortly after the Bubble burst, she obtained patents to supply Ireland and the American colonies with over £100,000 worth each of half-pence and farthings. She sold the patents to William Wood, who aimed to make a net profit of £36,000. The story got out and the subsequent uproar was known as the scandal of Wood's Half-pence. Sir Isaac Newton, Master of the Mint, certified the coinage, but at this point in his maverick career Jonathan Swift turned Tory. He penned a vitriolic attack on the new ha'pennies, causing the Irish Parliament to discredit the coins. The English government was obliged to cancel the patents, and the Duchess was fiercely lampooned. No blue plaque commemorates her stay in Grosvenor Square, and to add insult to injury her portrait does not even appear in the Britannia Hotel's collection of memorabilia.

For the next two centuries the charm and dignity of Sir Richard's square acted like a magnet to the English aristocracy. In the 1730s ten earls, two marquesses, the Duke of Manchester, the Dowager Duchess of Rutland and the Bishop of Durham all went to live there. By the 1760s it had become a favourite spot for Prime Ministers. Lords Rockingham, Grafton and North all had houses in the square. In 1765 the otherwise undistinguished Duke of Bolton shot himself at No 37. In the nineteenth century, attracted by the spacious rooms which make such a pretty background for ancestral portraits, duchesses poured in. Soon so many portraits were lining so many panelled rooms, that the Square had become 'the very focal point of feudal grandeur'. There were also a good many horse paintings, for the further the English depart from their country seats, the more homesick they become, so they commission portraits of favourite animals to lessen the pangs of separation.

At the turn of the century coronets abounded. They were on the stationery and emblazoned on the sides of carriages. Everybody who was anybody had them on the silver and a few grandees still kept liveried footmen with gold embroidered insignia, front and back. Even in 1934 during the Great Slump, when so many large houses were converted into flats, Arthur Dasent was still able to describe Grosvenor Square as 'strewn with strawberry leaves and the blue ribbons of 'garter knights', for the residents included the Duke of Portland, the Marquess of Bath, the Dowager Duchesses of Somerset and Westminster, Lord and Lady Illingworth (the last couple to own a whole private house in the square) and a roving pack of MPs.

4
The Flat That Never Was

During the Second World War most of the north side of Grosvenor Square was requisitioned by the American Navy. When they left, an enterprising Czechoslovakian bought No 15. There had been a great deal of bomb damage, but the Czech hit on a scheme to lure back the duchesses.

Rafaelle, Duchess of Leinster, had been married before the War to the dashing but spendthrift Edward Fitzgerald, who sold his life interest in Carton, that gem of Irish Georgian architecture, which Desmond Guinness has spent a lifetime restoring. Fitzgerald had not expected to become Duke of Leinster, as he had two older brothers, Lord Maurice and Lord Desmond Fitzgerald. Consequently, Edward never thought he would live at Carton and accepted £130,000 plus an annuity for life of £1,000 from the financier, Sir Harry Mallaby-Deeley. Lord Maurice Fitzgerald died and Lord Desmond was killed in action in the First World War. Edward succeeded to the dukedom with nothing but a title and his £1,000 a year, since he had already spent the £130,000 during his first marriage to the actress May Ethridge. As a Duke, Fitzgerald naturally wished to buy back his inheritance, so Mallaby-Deeley, who was something of a sportsman, sponsored him to sail for New York in search of an heiress.

No discretion surrounded this arrangement and the gossip columnists freely proclaimed Edward's availability, so that in America he was warmly received by the best society. A British duke, free of matrimonial ties, just what every American debutante dreams about! Before leaving London his Grace had been guest of honour at a huge private luncheon given by some lively Americans at Claridges. One of the guests was Mrs Clare Van Neck, the former Rafaelle Kennedy, who had charmed London society in the twenties with her Parisian clothes, her emerald green fan and her jewelled bandeaux. Unfortunately most of the jewels were paste and the Brooklyn-born beauty, famed for her devastating frankness, was the first to admit it.

The Van Neck marriage had not been a success. Rafaelle wore white and carried a bouquet of orchids and lily of the valley. Her impression of the guests was that most of them had dressed in the drawing room curtains and to the end of her days she referred to Eaton Place, where the couple set up home, as 'Dead Man's Gulch'. Edward wooed and won Rafaelle, whom he spotted eating pancakes in Child's Restaurant, as soon as he reached New York. He saved her from a life of boredom on the grouse moor, for she was not a keen sportswoman. Though temporarily dazzled by Van Neck, she found his attractions waned when she finally realised the reason they were invited everywhere was not because she wore Worth dresses, but because he was 'a jolly good shot'.

She fell, almost literally, from the frying pan into the fire. Edward's chief passion was driving high-powered motor cars at illegally high speeds. There was little money and their relationship was punctuated by exciting episodes, fleeing from his creditors. When the newly married Duke and Duchess went back to Carton the Fitzgerald household lined up outside the house, while the town band played 'America, my America'. The servants imagined Lord Edward was bringing home a second Barbara Hutton, that logs would crackle again in the massive hearths and the sixty bedrooms would be electrically lit and re-curtained – all with the dollars which the new Duchess did not have.

When there really was no money left, Edward left her, but Rafaelle had the will to succeed. She never forgot that, briefly, she had been Ireland's premier duchess. As Mrs Van Neck she had been presented to Queen Mary in a dress of misty blue by Norman Hartnell. As Duchess of Leinster she was presented by Edward's aunt, the beautiful Helen d'Abernon, to Queen Elizabeth, this time in a dress by Schiaparelli with a diamond tiara and an emerald green train. By an enormous stroke of good fortune, Rafaelle was best friends with Princess Maud, the daughter of the Princess Royal, 'Maudie' was married to Lord Carnegie and prospective chatelaine of Kinnaird Castle. This meant that, when Edward abandoned her, the Duchess was able to fall back artfully on a network of good connections. She spent a useful War in America, running Bundles for Britain, an organisation which sent food parcels to prisoners of war. When she returned to London she had set her heart on a flat in Grosvenor Square.

Before the War she had fallen in love with a flat at No 15. It was in her thoughts as she booked rooms at the Dorchester and before she had finished unpacking her suitcases, the telephone rang. The Czechoslovakian entrepreneur seemed to have a sixth sense that the Duchess was back in London. He invited her to view No 15, the very apartment she craved. The whole building had been turned into a series of partitioned offices and although the US Navy had not yet vacated the premises, the enterprising Czech promised Rafaelle she could have it for £350 a year, as soon as the Navy moved out. Delighted, she returned to the Dorchester. Three months later the Czech gentleman rang to say Sir Harold and Lady Zia Wherner had taken the flat beneath Rafaelle's. They wanted to rent the Duchess's flat to use as servants' quarters. Now most people who knew Lady Zia will understand what happened next. Hers was a Fabergé-light touch, but she was the grand-daughter of a Russian Grand Duke and her requests brooked no denial. Would the Duchess, asked the Czech politely, consider the flat two floors above? It was identical. The Duchess consented, but a few days later she ran into a US naval officer with access to the building and together they went to see the flat above the Wherners. It didn't exist. The cunning Czech, having made it known that the Duchess of Leinster had taken premises at No 15, had then lured two other Duchesses to take apartments there.

Rafaelle paid a call on the wily Czech and in her own words she 'let him have it'. Cringeing, he offered her a flat on the sixth floor. It was servants' quarters but had six windows and a panoramic view of St Paul's and the Duchess sensed its possibilities. She took the flat and had her solicitor draw up not one, but a whole series of leases. By the time she died, priorities in the property market had been turned upside down.

During her last years she was the sitting tenant of one of the most desirable penthouses in all London.

5
Till Debts Us Do Part

A high-ranking lady with no need of a *pied-à-terre* in Grosvenor Square was Georgiana, wife of the fifth Duke of Devonshire. When she was seven years old, her father, Lord Spencer, moved into his new house in St James's. The Spencer fortune derived from Queen Anne's crony, Sarah Churchill, Duchess of Marlborough, widow of the victor of Blenheim. As the great Duke died without heirs male, the title passed through his daughter to her oldest son Charles, who inherited Blenheim Palace. He displeased the old Duchess, who promptly left a million pounds to his younger brother, the Hon John Spencer, Georgiana's grandfather. Sarah Marlborough thought the Spencers lacked political acumen and specified in her will that John should not accept a government post. This left the family with a lot of time on their hands and a passion for playing cards.

Georgiana's father became an antique collector. He travelled energetically between England and Italy, bringing home shiploads of classical statuary. When Althorp was no longer big enough to house all the Greek gods, marble nymphs and Roman Emperors, Lord Spencer built a London house to accommodate the overflow, as well as his wife and children. Georgiana was seventeen when her parents arranged the match with Devonshire. The fifth Duke was the richest man in England and she would be able to live quite near the Spencers at Devonshire House, just along Piccadilly. It had been beautifully modernised, since the days when the first Duke had acquired it from Lady Berkeley. Georgiana could also take her pick of the Duke's other properties, Chatsworth, Hardwick House, Bolton Abbey, Burlington House (which was practically next door to Devonshire House) and, prettiest of all, Chiswick House, the enchanting pavilion built by the discriminating Lord Burlington a few miles out of town and where, nowadays, the Hogarth Roundabout points the way to the M3.

It was an *embarras de richesse* for the giddy débutante about to marry London's most eligible bachelor. The gossips forecast doom and disaster, for many thought William Cavendish, the fifth Duke, the dullest and most unfeeling man in the realm. He was also a bad dancer. The wedding took place in June 1774, secretly, so that the couple would not be overwhelmed by curious spectators. The bride wore a white and gold dress, silver slippers and pearl drops in her hair. Her trousseau included sixty-five pairs of shoes, forty-eight pairs of stockings and twenty-six and a half pairs of gloves – perhaps the half was a spare in case the Duchess should turn out scatter-brained and leave her things behind. In the first three weeks after the wedding, she was expected to pay calls on around 500 persons of ton.

Everyone loved Georgiana. She was an instant success in Society, exhibiting the same star quality as her descendant, the late Diana, Princess of Wales. Georgiana had about £4,000 a year pin money. She was expected to spend lavishly upon hats and *coiffures*, entertainments, balls and interior decorators. Unfortunately the Cavendishes did not realise that they had welcomed a compulsive gambler into their midst. From earliest childhood Georgiana had watched her parents and their guests lose huge sums at faro. Her mother, Lady Spencer, constantly warned her against extravagance, advising her to stick to commerce, a game played by old ladies and country parsons. Sadly the Spencers did not practise what they preached. Their three oldest children, Georgiana, George and Harriet had been allowed to stay up till past midnight, watching the gambling at Althorp and Spencer House. On a family holiday in Paris, Harriet once wrote in her diary, 'A man came today to papa to teach how he might always win at Pharo, telling all his rules and that his secret was infallible.' Either the man was a charlatan, or Lord Spencer misunderstood the system, for when he died his widow discovered the family income was a quarter of what she expected. Most of it had been lost at the gaming tables. Nevertheless Georgiana had supportive parents. In the early part of her marriage, when her debts reached £3,000 (about

£180,000 in today's money) they settled them for her, merely advising her to reveal everything to the Duke.

The problem was that Georgiana lived so fast and furiously, she could seldom remember *everything*. Her debts were the most magnificent in London you understand, not petty bourgeois sums to be reckoned like beads on an abacus. She told the Duke about the sums she could remember, and optimistically assumed she would win enough at the next night's play to cover the difference. Tearful scenes followed and Georgiana promised reform. This became an established pattern of life in the Cavendish household, but when the Duchess's debts reached the £100,000 mark (around six million in today's terms) the Duke threatened divorce. As Georgiana was not brilliant at arithmetic the true sum was in fact somewhat larger. To conceal the facts she borrowed from everyone she knew including Thomas Coutts, her despairing banker, and the Prince of Wales, whose entire annual income amounted to only half of what Georgiana owed. Her credit had sunk so low that when the Prince and the Duke of Rutland began a new faro bank, she had to beg to join the consortium, but such was her sweetness and charm, the other members felt she could not be left out.

As the leader of Whig Society the Duchess also took an active part in party politics. At the Westminster elections of 1784 the ladies wore fox tails in their hats to show that they were supporters of Charles James Fox. The Whig candidate was a close friend and gambling crony of the Prince of Wales. George III, who detested his eldest son, told his Prime Minister, William Pitt, that he wanted Fox 'out at all costs'. England had just lost the American colonies, but anxious to gloss over such an unfortunate occurrence, the Tories brought in Admiral Hood, a terrific war hero to contest Fox's seat. The Whig ladies joined the men on the hustings led by the astonishing Duchess, who went into the taverns canvassing for Fox. She exchanged kisses for votes and was satirised unmercifully by the *Morning Post*, the scurrilous forerunner of the *Daily Telegraph*. When Pitt and the Tories prevailed, the Whigs paraded down Piccadilly, dressed in blue and buff, and formed a grand procession with their carriages. The Prince of Wales gave a *fête champêtre* at Carlton House, playing dance music so loudly that it ruined the dignity of the royal cavalcade when the King went to open Parliament. The Whigs were not suppressed and Devonshire House remained the focal point of Whig dissent for years to come.

Surrounded by a brilliant but dissipated coterie, the Duchess continued her gambling. The more she spent, the more she drove her Duke into the willing arms of her best friend, Lady Elizabeth Foster, who bore him two illegitimate children. As Georgiana had a generous and tolerant nature, and as she loved Bess, as she called Lady Elizabeth, as much as she loved her husband, the friends settled into a *ménage à trois*, which rotated between London, Chatsworth and Bath, except when Bess became pregnant and had to go abroad. Eventually after some desultory flirtation with the Duke of Dorset, Georgiana began a passionate affair with Lord Grey, which was blessed with issue. When she was six months pregnant, she told the Duke. Equality of the sexes was not a notion which crossed his mind, despite his continuing liaison with Lady Elizabeth and a previous fling, which he had conducted with the notorious Lady Jersey. In the eighteenth century sauce for the gander definitely differed from sauce for the goose. In a cold fury the fifth Duke banished his Duchess to France, which was on the verge of revolution, forbidding her to see her three legitimate children and severely limiting her cash flow. Modern biographers believe this did irreparable harm to his son and heir, the two year-old Marquis of Hartington, who wailed inconsolably 'Mama gone, Mama gone'.

As no one could bear to see Georgiana so painfully humiliated, her mother, her sister, Harriet Ponsonby, her brother-in-law, Lord Duncannon and their child Caroline went with her. At Georgiana's request the Duke's mistress and his illegitimate daughter, Caroline St Jules, were also of the party. They travelled to Nice, Italy and Switzerland, warmly welcomed as celebrities wherever they went. Georgiana stopped gambling and took up mineralogy. In Naples the party were guests of the British Ambassador, Sir William Hamilton and his wife, Emma, who was soon to make history as Nelson's mistress. At the time of Georgiana's visit Lady Hamilton had just begun to practise her 'attitudes', which were to prove such a hit with the painter Romney. In the flimsiest of draperies she would pose as a nymph or goddess in some lewd classical tale and sometimes, to heighten the effect, a servant would throw a bucket of water over her, so that the drapery clung to define her nipples.

After a number of adventures the party returned to England in 1793. The forgiving Duke welcomed them at Dartford, presenting Georgiana with an elegant new carriage, panelled in powder blue and embellished with silver springs. Back in Piccadilly, the entire Cavendish household was lined up in the courtyard as the Duchess swept through the gates of Devonshire House, looking for all the world as though she had come back from the Grand Tour.

Georgiana was much mellowed by her exile, but one member of the party who had travelled to Naples was soon to become the new wild child of Mayfair society. Caroline Ponsonby, the Duchess's niece had gone away an ill-mannered little girl, whom Lady Spencer had had to chastise for being rude to the great historian Edward Gibbon. 'She is very naughty and says anything that comes into her head,' wrote Georgiana, who believed that at seven Caroline should have received a good slapping. 'She told poor Mr Gibbon, who has the misfortune of being very ugly that his big face frightened the little puppy with whom he was playing.' By 1803 Caroline was a wayward young beauty, presented at Court along with her cousin, the Devonshires' daughter, Harriet Cavendish. Caroline Ponsonby was soon to embark on a romance which would make her mother and aunt look like a brace of respectable dowagers.

6
Dangerous to Know

Nobody in the Devonshire House circle ever seemed to call Lady Caroline Ponsonby by her full name. To the family she was always 'Caro', to distinguish her from the Duke's illegitimate daughter by Lady Elizabeth Foster, Caroline St Jules. To avoid scandal the resourceful Bess had persuaded an elderly French Count to accept her daughter's paternity, so the little girl was able to grow up beside her half sisters, Georgiana and Harriet Cavendish. The two Carolines spent a good deal of time in each other's company during the Duchess's long sojourn abroad. Caro Ponsonby always knew how to make herself the centre of attention and, although she was a naughty child, she had winning ways and seems to have been easily forgiven. She was just two months older than her cousin, Lady Harriet Cavendish, and they were presented at Court together soon after England declared war on France in 1803. To avoid confusion with her aunt, Lady Bessborough, Harriet was known as 'Harryo'.

She and 'Caro' set off from Devonshire House together to make their début before Queen Charlotte. Both wore the fashionable white muslin dresses with low necks and puffed sleeves, which had come over from France and left little to the imagination. Previously, when Harriet's older sister came out, the dowagers still wore hoops to stiffen their dresses, so that Queen Charlotte's Drawing Rooms were insufferable torture because no one could move or sit in the crush of bouffant skirts and gentlemen's swords. Periodically edicts were issued to ban hoops and swords at Court, but the great cages of whalebone beneath the ladies' petticoats hampered seduction and upheld the last vestiges of moral order. With the French Revolution and the revealing new gowns, a floodtide of libertarian values and

Romantic poetry swept Europe – as well as a most shocking new dance called the waltz.

Many thought it heralded a wave of overtly lascivious conduct. Byron wrote a poem about it, a much neglected work beginning:

Muse of the many-twinkling feet! whose charms
Are now extended up from legs to arms.

It describes, hilariously, the frissons which ran through the ballrooms of Mayfair as mothers watched their uncorseted daughters take partners in the 'waltz hold'. Instead of the decorous touching of fingers, allowed by the minuet, the lady now placed her hands on the gentleman's shoulder, while he encircled her waist with his arms. The couple danced face to face and hip to thigh. Byron thought it more than human flesh could stand. Other dances like Scottish reels and the Irish jig required skilled footwork but,

Waltz – waltz alone – both legs and arms demands
Liberal of feet and lavish of her hands;
Hands which may freely range in public sight
Where ne'er before – but – pray put out the light.

If the ladies were not careful, their puff sleeves slipped and their delicate bosoms peeped over the top of the flimsy, low-cut dresses. Not only did the chemise replace hoops and stays, women wore their hair à la Grecque, in swept-up classical styles in imitation of the Empress Josephine. Out went powder and wigs, in came a close-cropped boyish look, which was very fetching on a young beauty with natural curls. Caro's mother had set the latest style for male beauty when she took Lord Leveson Gower as her lover. He was the very paragon of the new look, with large brown eyes and soft curly hair, flicked forward at the temple, but cut short at the back to allow room for a fastidiously tied cravat to sit properly. Both the Prince Regent and Beau Brummell affected the Romantic new hairstyle, but it was to find its apotheosis in Lord Byron, who glowered histrionically from beneath his chestnut locks.

Shortly after her Season, Caro Ponsonby married William Lamb, later Queen Victoria's Prime Minister, but at the beginning of the nineteenth century a quiet young gentleman, very much under the thumb of his fascinating, unprincipled mother, Lady Melbourne. Melbourne House was along Piccadilly, just beyond Burlington House, and it was almost the only house south of Oxford Street which had not been decorated by the fashionable Adam brothers. It was a magnificent classical pile, designed by William Chambers, who was about to start on Somerset House. The grand salon was fifty-two feet long, Chippendale made the furniture, and the celebrated Florentine artist Giovanni Cipriani decorated the ceilings. Lord Melbourne spent £100,000 on his house and Lady Melbourne entertained there in a style which rivalled Georgiana's. She was not short of lovers, and it was said of her that 'she understood the art of getting on with men completely', for Lady Melbourne had the gift of discretion. As Caro's mother-in-law she must have felt much as Lady Spencer and Georgiana did, when the naughty child was rude to Mr Gibbon.

As the world knows, from the moment Caroline Lamb met Byron the pair were passionately attracted. She wrote in her diary, 'Mad, bad and dangerous to know'. Generations of women have thrilled to the sentiment ever since. Byron wrote her a few desultory poems. He had published the first two cantos of *Childe Harold's Pilgrimage* in 1812 and woke one morning to find himself famous. Women fell for him in droves. They wrote him sentimental letters and swooned at his feet. Caro, for him, was a passing fancy. She had literary aspirations herself, so was scarcely the type to minister as an all-comforting Muse. As her behaviour grew more eccentric, he rejected her more coldly. She was frantic to regain his attention. She burst into his rooms disguised as a page boy. On one occasion she took him by surprise, scrawling, 'Remember me' across the fly-leaf of a book which lay open on his writing desk. She was not only exhibitionistic, she had defaced the book. Byron dipped his pen in vitriol and screeched back words, which made all the best anthologies,

Remember thee! Remember thee!
Till Lethe quench Life's burning stream
Remorse and Shame shall cling to thee,
And haunt thee like a feverish dream!

Lady Caroline felt neither shame nor remorse. She made a bonfire of facsimiles of all the letters Byron ever wrote her and danced round it accompanied by local girls dressed in white. This performance was said to have taken place after she had written her first novel, *Glenarvon*, in which Byron was severely caricatured. He told Madame de Stael he didn't think much of it. 'If the authoress had written the truth,' he confided to Tom Moore, 'the romance would not only have been more romantic, but more entertaining. As for the likeness, the picture can't be good; I did not sit long enough.'

Hell hath no fury like a lady novelist scorned. Caro's revenge followed Byron to posterity, for far from sinking into obscurity, she set a fashion. Marriage had done little to change her wild behaviour. There is a story that once, at Devonshire House, she was carried in naked, concealed under a pie-crust, and sprang out upon the supper table before the astonished guests. She was thus the forerunner of the stripogram. The truth of the story is immaterial, it caught the imagination of future generations and assured her of a place in the *Dictionary of National Biography*. In 1972 she was the subject of a full-length feature film with Sarah Miles as the heroine and Richard Chamberlain as Byron. Nobody knows whether Caroline's love was consummated. The saddest epitaph of all came from J.B. Priestly, the author of scores of successful novels, whose West End play, *An Inspector Calls* is official Eng Lit on all the best GCSE syllabuses. Priestley, a blunt Yorkshireman, who was happily married to Jacquetta Hawkes, despite being the veteran of several amours, thought – pssst – that Byron and Caroline never even made love. So sad to think the passionate little creature was a blue-stocking all along, victimised by her own neurotic imaginings.

Had she been born into our own century of course, Lady Caroline would have had no time for sighing and longing. She would have been sent to a progressive nursery school to develop a healthy attitude to sex. Lord Byron would not have penned

Remember thee!. He would have sent her a copy of Dr Greer's *The Female Eunuch*, or even this season's *succès de scandale, The Whole Woman*, which offers us thirty-five self-contained chapterets of fiery rhetoric on Breasts, Girlpower, Mutilation, and somewhat puritanically, 'Sex and Sorrow'.

7
Little America

Let us suppose an observant tourist travels to Mayfair on a No 9 Bus. He takes the eastern approach, leaves behind the Royal Borough of Kensington and Chelsea and enters the City of Westminster via Hyde Park Corner. On his left he will spy a large dignified mansion, faced with Portland stone. It sits on its own private island, poised between Queen Elizabeth Gate and the entrance to the Park Lane Subway. A few years ago the No 9 bus conductor would have explained to our tourist that the big house was No 1, Piccadilly, or No 1 London, that it was the home of the Duke of Wellington, the great hero who defeated Napoleon at Waterloo and that the present Duke of Wellington still lives there. The building is called Apsley House and was purchased by the 'Iron Duke' with money voted to him by a nation, grateful to have been saved from Napoleon's grand design to make Britain part of Europe.

All this information the bus conductor would have offered free, explaining that Apsley House was called No 1 London because it was the first house after the Hyde Park toll gate. As a true Brit, regardless of whether he was black or white, he would have been proud to volunteer a bit of history. Nowadays bus conductors do not tell tourists about Apsley House. This is because on approaching Hyde Park Corner, a glazed expression passes over the features of your average London Transport official, as he prepares to intone the next destination – 'Hard Rock Café'.

Shortly after Waterloo a number of trophies were exhibited at No 1. The public queued to see the memorabilia, including Napoleon's coach, a portrait of Josephine in a nipple-skimming neckline, the Sèvres dinner service they used, and a colossal statue of the French Emperor, dressed à la Grecque in a fig leaf and a bit of drapery. At the time it was commissioned Napoleon, a small man with hunched shoulders and terrible deportment, said it was 'rather too athletic', but the British public queued and queued and Cruikshank did an unforgettable cartoon of them swarming over 'Boney's' coach and peeping in through its windows.

Several thousand visitors go to Apsley House each year. It was built by Robert Adam between 1771 and 1778, originally in red brick. The Portland stone was added afterwards to give a more ducal appearance. Mysteriously nowadays it is listed as 149, Piccadilly. Its railings are still painted a mellow, post-war green, which is a welcome change from the harsh black, now *de rigueur* for London's elegant wrought-iron work. There is never a queue outside Apsley House, but the Hard Rock Café is seldom without one. It was started 27 years ago by Isaac Tigrett and Pete Morton, two Americans who couldn't get a decent hamburger anywhere in London. The publicists reckon fifteen million customers must have passed through its doors since it first opened up in 1971. Its rock memorabilia collection began when Eric Clapton donated his guitar. Pete Townshend of The Who promptly presented his, and the collection now runs to 40,000 artefacts. As there is no room to display them all in one venue, they are rotated round the world to Hard Rock's 92 off-shoots. Almost every rock musician of note has played or eaten there and, rather unsuitably, Linda McCartney chose this temple of meat-eating to launch her new range of vegetarian food in 1991. The queue outside Hard Rock is a tribute to American marketing methods, but a large part of it is nowadays made up of globe-trotting grannies, who wish to collect Brownie points back home by importing Hard Rock T-shirts to the United States, as souvenirs of London.

Shortly before Adam built Apsley House, he designed a residence just off Piccadilly with large gardens for the third Earl of Bute. Choosing a site was complicated, because when the Duke of Devonshire became entangled in the Chancery case over the purchase of Berkeley House, he instructed his lawyers to draft a clause, whereby Lord Berkeley's heirs agreed not to build on the land they retained in any way which might annoy the Duke. This meant Adam had to slant his design diagonally across the area, where Curzon Street now sweeps round into Berkeley Square. Bute, who was George III's mentor, resigned from public office in 1763. He sold the half-finished property to Lord Shelburne and retired to Bedfordshire, where he built Luton Hoo. Shelburne, later the first Marquis of Lansdowne, signed the Treaty of Paris in the beautiful rotunda of what is now the Lansdowne Club. This ended the War of Independence and, not surprisingly, a steady flow of American members and guests drift into the Rotunda to gaze reverentially at the portrait of the first Marquis, robed in ermine and the framed copy of the Treaty. We Brits are tolerant of their presence and do not mention that the War is still listed in *The Companion to British History* as 'the American Rebellion'.

I will not go into the full story of how we lost the colonies. It is painful to relate and owing to the absence of television in the reign of George III, it has never been easy to divide it into proper episodes. One highlight was the Boston Tea Party, which brought things to a head in 1773. Lord North, who was yet another of George III's short-term advisers, disliked the job description 'Prime Minister', though he agreed to accept the office. He reformed the East India Company, reducing the price of tea. This annoyed the Boston merchants, who dressed their henchmen as Red Indians, sending them to raid a tea clipper. Its cargo was thrown into Boston Harbour. Lord North, shocked by the waste of tea, at a time when he was trying to economise by reducing the Royal Navy, threatened terrible reprisals. The other states backed Massachusetts, which came as a painful surprise. It shows how easy it is to develop a puffed-up sense of self-importance if you live in Grosvenor Square. Lord North simply did not understand the *nerve* of a man like George Washington.

Everyone was trying to keep the colonies happy. An earlier Prime Minister, Lord Rockingham, reduced the tax on French molasses, which kept down the price of Rhode Island rum. You would have thought it a popular move, but the New England puritans maintained it corrupted the garrison, causing the British troops to seduce their daughters. When the Declaration of Independence was made on 4 July, one signatory was John Adams, a Massachusetts lawyer. In 1785 they made him Minister to England. He metaphorically thumbed his nose at Lord North by establishing the first Yankee Embassy in Grosvenor Square. While he was in London, he wrote his *Defence of the Constitution of the United States.* Washington made him Vice-President. Englishmen thought it a poor return for lowering the rum prices. They tended to close their minds to what was happening across the water. Over 100 years later when Consuelo Vanderbilt, the nineteen year old American heiress, who became Duchess of Marlborough in 1895, met her mother-in-law, Lady Blandford, the latter thought all Americans lived on plantations with negro slaves and that Red Indians waited round every corner to scalp people.

Like many Americans, Consuelo was shocked by the stratification of English society. When she asked her butler to light an already laid fire, he replied with a grave bow, 'I will send the footman to your Grace,' to which she answered, 'Oh don't trouble, I will do it myself.' Having thrown off the constraints of a class system and founded a nation which oscillated between Republicanism and Democracy, the colonists soon began to hanker after the homeland. They made in droves for Mayfair and special hotels had to be built to accommodate them. Amid the open spaces of an almost empty continent, they had conceived the idea that 'big is beautiful', so they tried to make their mark in London by establishing colossi. One of the first buildings erected in Mayfair by an American was the Royal Institution, which Benjamin Thompson established as a vast lecture theatre for teaching 'the application of science to the common purposes of life'. Thompson was a New Englander, who had fought against Washington. George III knighted him and in 1800 granted the Institution a Royal Charter. Thirty years later Michael Faraday conducted his experiments in electricity there. The Royal Institution dominates Albemarle Street. It is so big that if you are stuck beside it in heavy traffic, you have to crane your neck out of a taxi to see the acanthus leaves at the top of the pillars.

The Chicago entrepreneur Gordon Selfridge also had a passion for Olympian grandeur. When he announced his intention of constructing an American-style store in Oxford Street, no one could believe that a mere shop could extend so far.

Thousands of people received invitations to the opening, which was heralded by a military fanfare. Behind the façade were eight floors, housing one hundred departments. Over 90,000 people went into Selfridges that day.

American wealth secured the best families homes in London. Waldorf Astor rented 54, Berkeley Square for the then astronomical sum of $25,000. Selfridge was the next occupant. He lavishly re-fitted the whole house while his shop was being built. Later he was to rent Lansdowne House itself. John Pierpont Morgan Junior moved into 12, Grosvenor Square. Waldorf's cousin, Ava Astor, took 18, Grosvenor Square. New York financiers began to subsidise London building schemes throughout the 1890s. Walter Hayes Burns, business partner to Pierpont Morgan, fused 69 and 71 Brook Street into one single extravaganza, with a ballroom and staircase resembling the set of a Viennese opera. It has since become the Savile Club, which was founded by a set of young men in the 1860s, who thought the conventions of St James's Street too stuffy. They took their name from their second premises in Savile Row and moved to Brook Street in 1928. The ballroom is powder blue with silver gilt mouldings. Little clouds chase each other across the ceilings and to dine there on Fridays, when ladies are admitted, and cherished by the inimitable Alfredo, is still one of the most frivolous delights which Mayfair affords.

That most English of hotels, the Ritz, now the only five star establishment in London which still boasts British ownership, was originally bitterly criticized as an American concept. The inhabitants of Berkeley Square, watching the gigantic new steel frame going up in 1904–5 – supervised by the American contractors, James Stewart & Co – complained it would damage their health by blocking the supply of fresh air from Green Park. It was the creation of César Ritz, the thirteenth child of an Alpine shepherd, who became the most renowned hotel manager in Europe. During the 1890s at the Savoy, Ritz revolutionized the concept of dining out, which the British considered vulgar, except when abroad. The cosmopolitan Swiss hired Johann Strauss to play in the restaurant, attracting the flower of Edwardian Society including the Prince of Wales and Lillie Langtry. Abetted by Lord Randolph Churchill this powerful coterie changed the licensing laws, which required drinking to cease at 11 pm. The Savoy restaurant stayed open until 12.30. Society flocked there, but Ritz never got on with the draconian housekeeper. When their quarrels reached a climax, he resigned and Escoffier, the world's most famous chef decamped with him. Messages of sympathy flowed in from the great and the good. The Prince of Wales said, 'Where Ritz goes, I go' and cancelled a party. A new consortium backed by the South African millionaire, Alfred Beit founded the Ritz in Paris. It was designed by the celebrated French architect Charles Mewès, who later came over to execute the brilliant interiors of the English Ritz, but although Mewès and his partner Arthur Davis created a replica of an eighteenth-century chateau, the folk from Berkeley Square never forgot the shock of the steel girders going up. They never forgave Mewès and Davis for the loss of their view of the Park, so for them the Ritz remained firmly 'American'.

The opening dinner in May 1906 was an eleven-course feast, featuring 1878 claret. Soon the élite of Europe came to stay. Opera and ballet stars rubbed shoulders with English Duchesses, Melba, Caruso, Diaghilev and Pavlova were patrons. The rosy glow of the Palm Court and the lovely painted dining room overlooking the Park drew all the wealth and elegance of Edwardian society. The rooms were the most expensive in London at a guinea a night.

Through the Edwardian period the American Embassy consisted of some shabby rooms near Victoria Station. In 1913 Walter H. Page, the new American Ambassador, moved his Chancery to No 6, Grosvenor Square. Like Consuelo Vanderbilt he was amazed by English servants. He wrote to his brother to describe how fifteen English servants do 'just about what seven good ones would' in the United States, but he was remarkably impressed by the way his staff knew everyone's names and titles, addressing people correctly as 'Your lordship', or 'Your Grace'. An English butler, Page reckoned, was 'a sort of duke downstairs', and, he reported astonished, 'that's worth more than money to an Old World servile mind.'

The following spring the Ambassador wrote to President Wilson. He commented on the guard who stood outside the

Bank of England, although it was now in a building which 'would withstand a siege'; that King Charles I's statue was hung with flowers on the anniversary of his death; that books were written 'about the mistresses of Kings – serious historical books!' 'Nothing is ever abolished, nothing ever changed . . . there is not a salesman in Piccadilly who does not wear a long tail coat.' The Ambassador was quite bowled over by our art of high living. When the English 'make their money,' he wrote, 'they stop money making and cultivate their minds and gardens . . . I guess they really believe that the earth belongs to them.'

As we have already explained in the story of Rafaelle, the Brooklyn-born Duchess of Leinster, Grosvenor Square suffered severe bomb damage in the Second World War. Some of the plane trees survived, but not the most beautiful buildings. A discreet notice in the gardens tells us that John Alston was the gardener after the War and that the square was re-structured in 1948, when the Ministry of Works took over management from the Grosvenor Estates. Since the 1930s, says the notice, the square has had a strong association with the United States of America. 'The present Chancery at No 24 was completed in 1960. The British Memorial to President Roosevelt was unveiled in 1958 and the Eagle Squadron monument erected in 1994.' The notice is tactful, it does not need to mention that No 24 covers the entire west side of Grosvenor Square; that it is widely regarded by the few remaining indigenous Brits as the birth-place of Thank-God-It's-Friday-Parties, and that architectural purists regard it as 'the greatest affront one great nation ever offered to another.' Still, we, who queue for visas to travel Virgin Atlantic, must not complain. The staff are polite and friendly and wish us to 'Have a nice day!'

There is one story which circulates widely and it has not been denied by the Grosvenor Estates. President Kennedy visited the great Chancery and commented that in all other countries the United States owned the territory upon which its embassies were built. Could he perhaps buy the freehold? The then Duke of Westminster, the flamboyant Bendor, was approached. Certainly, came the reply, the Duke would consider selling, if the United States would return the land which they had appropriated from the Grosvenor family at the time of the American Rebellion. Histories were speedily consulted and it was discovered that the Grosvenor territory had apparently included the site of Cape Canaveral. The Duke remained the freeholder.

In the days when Mayfair was full of American movie stars, the actress Rita Hayworth was dating Prince Aly Khan. It was rumoured his father, the Aga, might put in an appearance at a certain party. The nervous hostess consulted the College of Arms about her seating plan. She received the reply, 'The Aga Khan is held to be a direct descendant of God; a British duke takes precedence'.

8
'A Nightingale Sang'

Sir Max Beerbohm is credited with saying that there is 'very little squareness' about Berkeley Square, for it is a perfect oblong. The reasons once again hark back to the seventeenth century with its haphazard approach to Town and Country Planning. The leasing of Lady Berkeley's gardens, the Duke of Devonshire's clause binding her sons not to 'annoy' him and the erratic diagonal siting of Lansdowne House would never have been tolerated in an economy regulated by Brussels. The south side of the square remained undeveloped until the 1930s, when Devonshire House had been pulled down and the Duke's descendants could no longer be 'annoyed'. The east side was built before the west, but all authorities concur that No 44 on the west side, which William Kent designed for Lady Isabella Finch was, and is, one of the loveliest houses in Georgian London. It is now the Clermont Club, with Annabel's in the basement, and its proprietors have conserved and restored its treasures in a fitting manner.

Kent spent three years building No 44. One of its features is a staircase with a wrought-iron balustrade, which Horace Walpole described as the most 'beautiful piece of scenery' which could be imagined. It led to a landing with an Ionic colonnade of graceful proportions and, at the back of the house, to Lady Isabella's boudoir, a palatial confection of white and gold, appropriate to one who was Lady of the Bedchamber to George III's great aunt, the Princess Amelia. Kent's grand salon rose through two floors with dummy windows at the front to preserve the symmetry of the façade. The ceiling of Greek gods and goddesses at play was painted by Antonio Zucchi and the door and chimney pieces were carved from white and coloured marble decorated with winged cherubs, pouting in the Italian fashion. The whole place was so seething with foreign workmen, with painters and gilders, carvers and plasterers, that poor 'Lady Bell', as she was known in intimate memoirs of the time, could not move in until March 1744. She was rated at £2 3s 4d for the year and very properly refused to pay on the grounds she had not occupied the place a twelvemonth. In the end she paid up 10s.

Lady Isabella was the seventh daughter of a seventh Earl, the Earl of Winchilsea. She had an unfashionably dark complexion, which may have been one of the reasons she died a spinster, but hers was an independent nature and she suffered from a tendency to make pert remarks. The Earl of Bath, who was immensely rich, once lost half a crown to her at cards, when he was 74 years old. He sent the money round next day, apologising that he could not give her a crown (five shillings). She replied that if he chose to give her a coronet, by proposing marriage, she would willingly accept. Horace Walpole, who lived at the opposite side of the square at No 11, frequently attended Lady Bell's *soirées*. He kept up a stream of witty, if ungentlemanly, allusions to her dark complexion and spied on the grand people going in and out of her house, who included most members of the Royal Family.

Princess Amelia never married either. She was betrothed in youth to Frederick the Great, who wrote affectionate letters to her until she was twenty-three, when he married another. When Amelia died, they found a portrait miniature of Frederick round her neck. She paid for the equestrian statue of George III which stood at the centre of Berkeley Square. It was put up just about the time when the gilding, which had so delighted the Duchess of Kendal, was wearing thin on the statue of George I in Grosvenor Square. George III was designed by an eminent French sculptor, Baupré, in 1772. This time the reigning monarch was not gilded. He was fashioned from decent bronze, but clad, rather unsuitably, as Marcus Aurelius. Some fifty years later, the delicate legs of his horse buckled under the weight of the imperially robed rider and he was replaced in 1827 by the present gazebo.

Some of the plane trees in Berkeley Square were planted in

1789. The date is coincidental and not connected with the French Revolution, or the dreadful fervour of the Paris mob, who stormed the Bastille on 14 July. The London planes were planted by Edward Bouverie, who lived at No 13, next to Horace Walpole on the east side. They have stood sentinel over the grassy sward for over two hundred years, gracefully enhancing the dignity of the square, which even the roar of present-day traffic cannot mar.

Devonshire House itself, chief cause of the square's delayed completion, was set back from Piccadilly with a great wall at the front to preserve the privacy of the Cavendishes. Its gardens were full of elm trees and classical statuary. At the back of the house, the Duke's territory was screened from the square by the luxuriant gardens of the Marquis of Lansdowne. The Tyburn flowed between the two properties, marking a natural boundary. It was not, by the 1760s, exactly a purling stream. Like any open waterway in that part of London it was used for refuse. A parish register of 1753 describes the river as 'a Common Sewer', which was an unpleasant thing to find on the perimeters of land owned by a Duke and a Marquis. This may explain why Lord Lansdowne hastened to plant sweet scented lilacs on the south side of his garden. Lansdowne Passage, a sinister footpath, ran below street level following the course of the Tyburn. Technically the passage was the property of the Marquis, who closed it to the public one day a year to preserve his rights. The other 364 days it was a general thoroughfare, approached by steps at either end. Dank and unhygenic, it was often the scene of violent crime and connected Curzon Street with Berkeley Street. After a highwayman escaped the gallows by riding his horse down the steps and looping back into Piccadilly to evade his pursuers, a vertical iron bar was placed at one end to prevent further equestrian feats. All of this occurred beneath the stupefied gaze of the Secretary of State for Foreign Affairs, Thomas Grenville, who watched the chase from his window. The historic steps are said to survive as a kitchen exit from the Mayfair Inter-Continental Hotel.

In the 1740s when the east side of Berkeley Square was settled and the west still under construction, some desultory planting was attempted in the space between them. By 1766 this

. . . a highwayman escaped the gallows by riding his horse down the steps and looping back into Piccadilly to evade his pursuers . . .

had fallen into horrible neglect. An Act of Parliament provided for the laying out of a proper garden supervised by a Board of Trustees, a sure sign of the superior nature of the square's residents. A year later 'iron pallisadoes' enclosed the grass plots and gravel walks, which are now such a familiar part of the Mayfair scene and the plane trees growing to maturity enhanced the sylvan effect. In short Berkeley Square in the late eighteenth century, with its wooded environs and the Marquis's adjacent lilac walks, was just the sort of place where you might have expected to hear a nightingale sing, but apparently none did. Even Horace Walpole, who never missed a thing, didn't hear one.

Walpole had read classics at King's College, Cambridge, and when he moved to No 11, he so enthused over the view, that he was moved to compare the statue of George III to a work by the Athenian sculptor, Phidias. Obviously, this tremendous piece of humbug was designed to get him an invitation to one of Lady Isabella's card parties at which Princess Amelia would be present, for everyone knows that when he made the Grand Tour in company with the poet, Thomas Gray, Walpole, the Father of Strawberry Hill Gothic, only got as far as Italy. Clearly the man hadn't set eyes on a work by Phidias in his life. When the horse's legs collapsed so ignominiously under King George, the statue was scrapped, but some thirty years later the third Marquis of Lansdowne commissioned the Victorian sculptor, Alexander Munro, to carve a nymph with a water vase out of white Carrara marble to decorate the square instead. She was intended as a drinking fountain. At first she stood outside the railings, dispensing water to thirsty passers-by. A pump concealed in the gazebo supplied her vase, through lead piping hidden under the gravel path. The scantily-clad lady did not always command the respect she deserved, however, so that she soon had to be moved to a secure position inside the railings. There the delicacy of her drapery and the sweet compassion of her expression could be admired by the ladies and gentlemen of the select milieu, which met under the plane trees. So beautifully was she carved that many mistook her for an antique goddess from the priceless collection assembled by the First Marquis. Time and weathering have eroded her once perfect

figure and recently she has met with a new indignity. On reno-
vating the pumping mechanism in 1994, Westminster Council
discovered impurities in the water. Publishing the news to avoid
a clash with health authorities, which nowadays means Brussels,
they lapsed into Department of Environment prose, describing
the poor nymph as 'a water feature'. In the days when Phidias
reigned as style guru of fifth-century Athens, Zeus would have
hurled a thunderbolt for less.

Even before Horace Walpole moved into No 11, 7 Berkeley
Square had been taken by Domenicus Negri, an Italian pastry
cook who started a tea room under the 'sign of the Pineapple'.
Fifteen years later he went into partnership with the entrepre-
neurial Mr Gunter. Gunter's, who soon became London's top
party caterers, supplied not only delicious food, but part-time
staff to all the best families in town. Many distinguished patrons
had accounts. The Duke of Sussex, the mildest of Queen
Victoria's wicked uncles and a popular after dinner speaker, had
still not settled bills dating from the 1820s when he died in
1843, despite repeated applications to Kensington Palace.

It was a tradition of the house that those who went to
Gunter's to eat their famous water ices, should be served out in
the square under the trees. When chairs and tables were fully
occupied, waiters would dash about, serving the élite clientele,
as they sat in their crested barouches, or open landaus. Some
ices were made to secret recipes, including the famous white
currant sorbets immortalised in the novels of Mrs Catherine
Gore. An authoress of the 'Silver Fork School', she wrote sixty
novels, all chronicles of high life, written long before
Thackeray-and-the-BBC thought up the plot of *Vanity Fair*. Mrs
Gore's heroines shopped in Old Bond Street and were as virtuous as Barbara Cartland's a hundred years later. When it came
to marriage, they had that same high sense of social purpose. In
Pin Money the Duchess of Trimbletown told of a débutante who
had been the success of the Season, learns that the girl's mother
had married into trade. The young belle was the daughter of a
toilet soap manufacturer:

' "A soap boiler" cried the Duchess feeling for her salts, so
that she would not faint at the thought of such a mesalliance, "It
is the pride of my life that not one of my daughters was allowed

to marry lower than an earldom."' Mrs Gore wrote of a Mayfair which had almost vanished by the 1820s, when Nathan Rothschild, the banker, was already hiring Gunter's staff to throw Fourth of July parties, openly celebrating Republican values in Piccadilly with champagne and lavish helpings of hothouse-grown pineapples.

Thackeray also looked back to an earlier decade for inspiration. In 1847, when he created his anti-heroine, Becky Sharp, she was a hussy of the first order, who had picked up false values in the aftermath of the Napoleonic Wars. Decked in jewels, paid for by the lecherous Marquis of Steyne, while her husband languishes in a debtor's prison, she was supposed to represent the worst vices of Mayfair womanhood. It is strange that in our own time *Harpers & Queen* consider Thackeray's bad girl such a successful go-getter that they set up a journalist with a £2,000 yellow coat by Gianni Versace to see if she could snare a millionaire in a modern replay of Becky's tactics.

Thackeray wrote from Kensington, but he knew Mayfair like the back of his hand. Becky, a.k.a. Mrs Rawdon Crawley, lived in Curzon Street, while her sister-in-law had a bow-fronted villa in Park Lane. However, no one who has read, studied, or lectured on *Vanity Fair* has ever been able to agree whether Chapter Forty-Nine in which Becky achieves her social ambitions triumphing over Lady Steyne and Lady Bareacres, takes place in Hanover, Grosvenor, or Berkeley Square, but a great deal of good claret and fine port has been expended discussing the issue. Perhaps Thackeray thought the Duke of Devonshire might sue for libel, or maybe he feared he would be cut at the Athenaeum. He coyly opted for a pseudonym, setting Gaunt House in Gaunt Square, which has perplexed literary detectives ever since.

In the annals of fallen womanhood worse was to come. In 1924 a young Armenian-born novelist, Michael Arlen, wrote *The Green Hat*. An unchallenged bestseller in its day, it went through seventeen impressions before the end of 1926. It is the tale of Iris Storm, who had 'a Chislehurst mind in a pagan body'. Mrs Storm, a self-confessed nymphomaniac, drives a yellow Hispanio-Suiza and inhabits a world in which Deauville and Trouville vie to be France's most fashionable resort. When in Mayfair, she goes nightly to the sort of parties which made the twenties 'roaring'. After sleeping casually with the narrator in Shepherd Market, she becomes pregnant by her girlhood sweetheart and loses the child in a Paris abortion clinic, where she almost dies of septic poisoning. All this is because her first husband, Boy Fenwick, throws himself off a balcony before consummating the marriage. 'Boy died for Purity' is a constant refrain of the book. Many people dismiss *The Green Hat* as trivial. It was said at the time that Michael Arlen, who wrote curious sentences inverting subject and predicate, was 'more Brilliantine than brilliant'. But the Bright Young Things did not despise *The Green Hat*. They concealed it from their Papas behind bound volumes of *Punch* and the *Collected Poems* of Rupert Brooke and they argued with their Mammas, who had read it surreptitiously, that 'Boy Fenwick died for purity'. The French shrugged. In Paris Schiaparelli brought out absinthe green hats, which were *un succès fou*. After all the nursing home of the abortion clinic was staffed by radiant nuns and received *une clientèle, la plus chic européene.* The relevance to Berkeley Square is that Michael Arlen's previous work, a collection of short stories called *These Charming People*, became a bestseller too and ran into eleven editions.

It was in the second short story in *These Charming People* that the nightingale indisputably sang. It was heard by 'a well-known poet, critic and commentator in 1921, the year of the drought'. In Arlen's story the poet-critic was 'distinctly sober', but learned ornithologists, who formed 'the St James's School of Thought', insisted that the nightingale did not sing. They also said, in the story of course, 'that the poet was not sober, or that he had heard a common thrush.' Now the important thing is not whether the wretched bird sang, or did not, nor yet whether the poet was drunk, or not, nor even, with the greatest deference to learned ornithologists and the St James's School of Thought, whether a nightingale had any business to be in Berkeley Square in the unbearably hot summer of 1921 with only the plane trees for cover. No, the important thing was that by giving life to the mythical bird, the trivial Arlen created a legend. An Armenian gave the 'immortal Bird' immortality, and he couldn't even write English with the subject and predicate in the proper places.

This said, 'When the Nightingale Sang in Berkeley Square' is a grim fable of a loveless marriage and a burning passion, which evaporates at the end of the story in a puff of smoke. The heroine is a Mayfair Madam of the worst type, the hero a cardboard figure of an Englishman, and the lover a neurotic egomaniac of the first order. The butler is the only wholesome human being in the entire piece, but the last sentences are lingering and poignant, like the smell of fresh lilacs in a silk-curtained drawing room:

> That was the night the nightingale sang in Berkeley Square. A nightingale has never sung in Berkeley Square before and may never sing there again, but if it does it will probably *mean* something.

Clever, canny, bold, clairvoyant and foreign Michael Arlen! By 1940 two young unknowns, Manning Sherwin the composer and Eric Maschwitz the lyricist, got together and wrote 'A Nightingale Sang', one of the most haunting songs of the Second World War and it echoed in the hearts of millions. The BBC played it. Glenn Miller made a best selling record. Vera Lynn, the Forces' Sweetheart, sang it and the girls dishing out steaming cups of NAAFI tea to the young men going to the Front hummed it, as did the nurses bandaging the young men who came back, and the girls in the MTC, who drove ambulances.

Those who danced to the tune seldom knew all the words. Many say London in the Blitz was 'like a holiday town', for the night clubs were mostly below street level, where people felt safe from the bombs. They were full of soldiers on leave. Wives and sweethearts flocked to the capital to meet them and the haunting refrain of the nightingale song seemed like a message of hope, even though Maschwitz's lyrics proclaimed it unlikely that any bird would sing in a Berkeley Square blacked out against air raids, its railings melted down in armaments factories, but the dancers didn't heed the words, they sang the tune. After the War there were seventy-four recordings and the little brown bird became a symbol of survival. A Nightingale Café opened in Lansdowne Row, and in the square a Nightingale Club. An unholy row broke out between the proprietors over who had first right to use the name.

A bustling, post-modernist St James's School of Thought survived the War. So did the learned ornithologists, who regularly fax the Editor of *The Times*, when they hear the first cuckoo of spring. They worry dreadfully about the National Decline in Spotted Flycatchers, but if you sit, dear Reader, on a May evening at about 6.30 facing Mr Maggs the Bookseller with your back to the National Westminster Bank on one of the benches donated by people from all over the world, who love Berkeley Square, you will see pink bluebells growing round the base of the largest plane tree. If you choose a time when the main traffic has ceased and just before the smart crowd surges up to the Clermont Club and down to Annabel's, you may also see small brown birds swooping for twigs and fragments of tree bark. Pigeon feeding is banned, but among the feathered fraternity it is a well-known fact that Berkeley Square is renowned as a place to find nest-building materials. You may not hear a nightingale, but if you think you do, e-mail the Editor of *The Times*.

9
Heirs and Graces

By the 1890s Piccadilly was distinctly built up. Although Green Park swept verdantly towards Buckingham Palace on the south side, the north no longer offered a tree-lined panorama, enhanced by the gardens of the nobility and gentry. By the turn of the century New Money had crept in. Apsley House fully lived up to its name 'No 1 London', being joined to the rest of the street by Piccadilly Terrace. This stylish block was instantly nick-named 'Rothschild Row', when cohorts of the banking family moved there and did up the interiors in *fin de siècle* rococo.

Next, hidden discreetly behind a brick wall, came Gloucester House, a charming old Georgian mansion which once belonged to Lord Elgin, and where the celebrated marbles first went on display – prompting a joke from Lord Byron about Lord Elgin's stone house. The Duke of Gloucester then bought the property and early in her reign Queen Victoria used to visit her widowed aunt, the Duchess, there. When 'Aunt Gloucester' died child-less, she left the house to her nephew, Prince George, second Duke of Cambridge and the last man to hold the title of Commander-in-Chief of the British Army. The Duke's uncles had led scandalous lives, cohabiting openly with their mistresses, but his father, Adolphus, Duke of Cambridge, seventh child of George III was known as 'the Good Duke'. He had married respectably and fathered Prince George and our present Queen's great grandmother, Princess Mary, later Duchess of Teck.

Prince George became Duke of Cambridge after his father's death in 1850. Three years earlier the rash youth had secretly married a Miss Louisa Fairbrother, a pantomime actress best known for her performance as principal boy in *Sinbad the Sailor*.

The role obliged her to wear white tights, a striped jacket with a jewelled sword stuck through her belt and a moustache. In infancy Prince George had been heir to the throne of England for two months during 1819, just before his cousin Victoria was born. Descended from George III's fourth son, she took precedence. Now by 1847, when Miss Fairbrother came on the scene, Victoria had reigned ten years. She was the mother of five children, including the future Edward VII, so it simply slipped Prince George's mind that he was contravening the Royal Marriage Act by failing to ask the Sovereign's permission.

Victoria would almost certainly have withheld it. When she first came to the throne, it had been thought Prince George might propose to Victoria himself. To qualify for the ordeal, he had grown fresh whiskers to hide a crop of late adolescent pimples, but the cousins did not take to each other and the young Queen, who disliked George's pushy mother, the Duchess of Cambridge and a former Princess of Hesse-Cassel, wrote of her aunt, 'Infamous woman', in the royal diary. Ten years later, as a young matron and filled with Albert's primly Germanic ideals on protocol, she would scarcely have welcomed a professional *pantomime artiste* into the family. Amateur theatricals went on at Windsor Castle and Victoria and Albert were much addicted to dressing up. Indeed, Landseer painted them attired as Queen Philippa and Edward III for the Plantagenet Ball of 1842. Of course, the Ball was held to promote the textile industry, which could hardly have been said of Miss Fairbrother in white tights, appearing for *money* at Drury Lane.

After her marriage the Duke's bride left the stage and bore him three sons. She set up house in an enchanting little property, No 6 Queen Street, where she entertained her husband at weekends. She never risked Queen Victoria's disapproval by moving into Gloucester House, where the Duke, uniformed and bemedalled, carried out his official duties as Commander-in-Chief of the Army. On Sundays he would jump into his phaeton and drive himself down Curzon Street to be with his family, who all took the surname FitzGeorge. The only appearances the couple made together in public were at the Mayfair Chapel, which they attended regularly throughout the fifty years of their marriage.

The Chapel was one of a number of private establishments which sprang up in the eighteenth century. They were licensed for prayer and preaching but not for Holy Communion. Some, like the Grosvenor Chapel and the Berkeley Chapel, were for family worship and attracted very select congregations of peers and peeresses. The Berkeley was upholstered in pink velvet and dominated by an enormous stove, lit by a good coal fire, but the Mayfair Chapel became notorious as a London alternative to Gretna Green. Quick marriages could be arranged there at a guinea a time. It stood near the end of Curzon Street, and its most celebrated incumbent was Dr Keith.

Dr Keith had been appointed parson in 1734 and was soon doing a roaring trade in irregular marriages, charging an extra five shillings for the Certificates. The Chapel was in the parish of St George's, Hanover Square. Revenue from the marriages was supposed to go to the parish, but according to Horace Walpole it went straight into the parson's own pocket and he was growing as rich as a bishop. He advertised in the press, performing seven hundred weddings in the year 1742, while the Rector of St George's celebrated only forty. To end the scandal Dr Trebeck, who had been Rector of St George's for nearly twenty years, excommunicated Dr Keith. The impudent parson promptly published a notice excommunicating not only Dr Trebeck, but also the Bishop of London. For this outrage he was sent to the Fleet prison, but continued his business from there by having his assistants open the 'Little Chapel', which stood across the road from the Mayfair Chapel at the end of Trebeck Street. The 'firm' continued to advertise in the *London Gazette*, giving directions for reaching the Little Chapel from Piccadilly or St James's.

Probably the most famous marriage that took place was that of the Duke of Hamilton, who met the beautiful, but virtuous, Miss Gunning at a party at Lord Chesterfield's. It was love at first sight. Two days later the Duke, his libido getting the better of him, sent for a parson, for the lady would not go to bed with him without one. All this happened in the evening and the parson flatly refused to perform without a licence and a ring. Swearing that he would send for the Archbishop, the Duke finally hit on the idea of using a ring from the bed curtain and the pair were married in the Mayfair Chapel at midnight. In the end Mayfair marriages became such a grievance with heiresses succumbing to abduction on the day they came of age, their furious fathers pursuing them to London from all parts of the country, that Lord Hardwicke brought a bill to Parliament for a Marriage Act to put a stop to the lucrative practice. Dr Keith's assistants, however, carried on right up to Lady Day 1754, the day before the Act came into force, when sixty-one marriages were performed at the Little Chapel in twenty-four hours.

Lord Hardwicke's Act did not put an end to clandestine marriages, though it stemmed the flow. It was followed in 1772 by the much more serious Royal Marriage Act, forbidding members of the royal family to marry without the Sovereign's consent. This was brought in after George III discovered that two of his brothers, the Dukes of Gloucester and Cumberland, had married unsuitable ladies. The Duke of Gloucester lived in Park Lane and married a titled widow who, it emerged, was descended on her mother's side from a postman. The Duke of Cumberland married a commoner in a house in Hertford Street, not very far from the infamous Mayfair Chapel. With such examples to follow, it was scarcely surprising that the young Prince of Wales, the future George IV, continued the family tradition. The heir to the throne, however, went a step further than his uncles. He married a Roman Catholic.

At fifteen, it had been said of 'Prinny' by his tutor, that he would be 'either the most polished gentleman, or the most accomplished blackguard in Europe – possibly both'. Before he came of age he had a flamboyant affair with the actress, Mrs Mary Robinson, whom he saw as Perdita in *The Winter's Tale*. She hangs now in the Wallace Collection, having sat for Reynolds, Romney and Gainsborough. She wrote poetry but was chiefly remembered for her hats. Her debts cost George III £60,000. His allowance cut by his father, and doubled by Parliament, the Prince moved out of Buckingham Palace to Carlton House, a magnificent establishment with handy access to Crockford's and White's at the top of St James's and to Berry Bros, the wine merchants at the bottom. At the age of twenty-one 'Prinny' secretly married the widowed Maria Fitzherbert at her house in Park Street, Mayfair. It was a rash and passionate act and one which could have cost him the crown.

For a long time Mrs Fitzherbert made the Prince a happy man, but she never renounced the Catholic faith. Despite the couple's discretion rumours abounded, enraging the King and causing Prinny, after one shower of parental abuse, to retire to Brighton, which immediately became a magnet for Society. Eventually the Prince married Caroline of Brunswick with full solemnities and sired the Princess Charlotte, who was a joy to her grandparents and considered a desirable heiress to the throne by the entire British nation. When the Prince separated from Caroline whom he detested, he implored Mrs Fitzherbert to return to his bed. They had been married by an Anglican clergyman and, faced with a dilemma between Church and State, she appealed to the Pope. Without hesitation his Holiness ruled that she was the Prince of Wales's lawful wife. This meant that in the eyes of Catholic Europe the hugely popular Princess Charlotte was the fruit of a bigamous union which had been officially sanctioned by the Archbishop of Canterbury.

Perjury, meanwhile, had been committed on the Prince's behalf by Charles James Fox and the playwright Sheridan who, deeming it their patriotic duty to hush up 'L'affaire Fitzherbert', both swore in Parliament that Prinny's first marriage had never taken place. A relieved House of Commons voted £221,000 towards those debts that heirs to the throne are wont to pile up and the King threw in an extra £10,000. Hounded by the press and cartoonists, Mrs Fitzherbert moved from Park Street to Tilney Street, which must have been a welcome bolt-hole from the Royal Pavilion, the garish love nest the Prince built for her at Brighton. The full details of Prinny's first marriage were not revealed until 1905, when Edward VII gave permission for the sealed envelope, containing the wedding certificate, to be removed from Coutt's Bank, where it had been deposited 72 years earlier. The signatures of the witnesses had been cut out with a razor, but it was established beyond reasonable doubt that the Anglican clergyman who performed the ceremony had done so in return for a hefty bribe, immediately after his release from debtor's prison. Mrs Fitzherbert remained at Tilney Street until her death in 1837.

To her eternal credit she made no retaliation when the Prince dumped her for Lady Hertford shortly before he was made Regent. She was fastidious about laundry, died a Catholic and does not appear to have sent any soiled linen into safe-keeping with her mother.

During this turbulent period of English domestic history, which encompassed the madness of George III, the Battle of Waterloo and the unforgettable moment when a Queen of England (Caroline) was locked out of her own coronation, prime sites along Piccadilly were snatched up, whenever they fell free. This happened rarely, as the great landlords continued the practice pioneered by the Berkeleys and the Grosvenors of leasing, rather than selling, land. The Mayfair Chapel, meanwhile, had become a little *declassé*. With the lucrative trade in marriages curtailed, the incumbent had let out the basement as a wine cellar. Popular preachers continued to draw an audience, but the congregation cannot have been as well-heeled as in the eighteenth century, because when the ninth Duke of Marlborough went house-hunting in the south-west corner of Mayfair, his American bride, Consuelo Vanderbilt, described Shepherd Market as 'a slum'.

As the young couple had no London home and the Duke was going into politics, Consuelo's father, William K. Vanderbilt, offered them the money to build one. The Mayfair Chapel was demolished to make way for Sunderland House, an imposing grey stone building in the French eighteenth-century style. When the Marlboroughs were warned that it was bad luck to pull down a church, they gaily quoted the old rhyme,

Spirits below, spirits of wine
Spirits above, spirits Divine

comforting themselves with the idea that they were purifying the area by destroying the wine cellar. Teetotalism has never really caught on in Mayfair and moral superiority doesn't go down too well either. Ill-luck did befall the couple, whose marriage ended in a chilly divorce. Between the wars Sunderland House was hired out for charity balls, and in May 1941 when the Blitz was at its worst, it was hit by a bomb. A wild figure was seen silhouetted against the flames, shouting, 'This building is doomed. It was built on consecrated ground – the site of the Mayfair Chapel.'

10
French Lessons

In Curzon Street within living memory there was a building owned by the Messina brothers, a family of affable Maltese gangsters, who aimed to bring a little bit of Mediterranean zest to London life. The trade that went on in this building was the oldest profession in the world, a very venerable profession you might say, wholly in keeping with the aims of Cool Britannia, since it serves both to keep young women off the streets and is hugely profitable to BT. What was novel about the establishment in Curzon Street was that it advertised 'French Lessons' in a most unusual way. A live mannequin sat in the window under a neon sign, which flashed on and off. She was perfectly dressed and, like the fibreglass dummies in the elegant vitrines of Regent Street, she wore the latest fashion. The implication was that she advertised the wares within. Only, of course, it wasn't the clothes that she was out to promote.

The connection between sex and imported vice in the English mind is curious. From the time of the Crusades, when Turkish baths and attendant handmaids were brought back to these islands, steamy ideas flourished in Southwark, which soon became London's chief centre of commercial wickedness. Henry VII, whose thrice-married mother was something of a martinet, closed down all the London brothels in 1506. This proved impractical and twelve were re-opened in 1507. Henry VIII, who was a good deal more influenced by his saintly grandmother in childhood, and his long-suffering sixth wife in old age, than most people suppose, shut down the whole lot. Since he died a few months later, it was probably a last minute spiritual insurance policy, carried out in the hope of gaining extra consolations in Heaven. Prostitution promptly spread all over

London. It caught on like wildfire north of the River, especially in Eastcheap, scene of all those affecting little tête-à-têtes in Shakespeare between Sir John Falstaff and the cockney bawd, Doll Tearsheet. Oliver Cromwell effected another clean up, but with the Restoration and the return of French luxury goods to the English market, the profession received a great moral boost.

Nell Gwyn, the most charming and least rapacious of Charles II's mistresses, did more than any other practitioner to make the time-honoured trade respectable. With a house at 79 Pall Mall – which is the St James's side of Westminster and a dear little hunting box designed for her by Christopher Wren at Newmarket – she has, strictly speaking, no place in this memoir of Mayfair, but Nell Gwyn played such a cheerful and refreshing part in the history of English whoredom that we can scarcely leave her out. She apparently sold fish before she sold oranges and she first set eyes on Charles II on the occasion of his marriage to Catherine of Braganza. Nell was twelve years old at the time, and amid the frenzied rejoicing with which the Londoners celebrated the royal nuptials, she ceded her own virginity to a city merchant. Soon afterwards she gained employment as a bar maid at the Cock and Pie tavern which was near the King's Playhouse in Covent Garden. After going there on work experience as an orange seller, she rose to become an actress and was soon playing comedy leads and sleeping with her co-star, Charles Hart, who, since she could not read, taught her her lines. At 16 she became the mistress of Lord Buckhurst, who treated her badly and at 18 of the King, who treated her well. Nell was adored by the Londoners for her good humour and great frankness. When the mob stoned her coach, thinking it to be that of her rival, Louise de Keroualle, Duchess of Portsmouth, whom everyone believed to be a french spy, Nell stuck her head out of the window shouting, 'Stop you fools, I am the Protestant whore not the Catholic one.'

A deeply sincere member of the Church of England, she had the words, 'Fear God, Serve the King' inscribed on her warming pan and performed her duties as a royal mistress with professional pride. Although reading and writing were never her forte, she took pains to acquire a smattering of culture and sat several times for Sir Peter Lely in various stages of classical

'Stop you fools, I am the Protestant whore not the Catholic one.'

undress. In one particularly charming study she posed as Venus in a little bit of chiffon, tossed across her thighs, while her infant son stood nearby in the role of a pensive Cupid. Her one chagrin was that the boy was only Earl of Burford, while all the other royal bastards were made Dukes. Madame de Sévingné, with her uncanny knack of seeing into another person's mind, wrote of the rivalry between Louise and Nell: 'She has a son by the King and wishes to have him acknowledged: she reasons thus: "This Duchess" says she, "pretends to be a person of quality; she says she is related to the best families in France; if she be a lady of such quality, why does she demean herself to be a courtesan. She ought to be ashamed of herself. As for me it is my profession. I do not pretend to be anything better." '

This unpretentious streak in Nell appealed greatly to the King. He made her son Duke of St Albans, so that the boy could hold his head high among the other royal bastards, the Dukes of Grafton, Northumberland, Southampton and Richmond. On his death bed in a famous aside Charles begged his brother, James, who was his successor, 'not to let poor Nelly starve'. Of his three mistresses, she kept the best table, understanding perfectly that the way to a man's heart was through his stomach. The King liked to sit up in bed devouring the pigeon pies which were one of her cook's specialities. He would wash these down with a prodigious amount of canary wine and wake refreshed to tackle the cares of State. Louise gave more sumptuous banquets, often in apartments more expensively furnished than those of the Queen, but her ideas on after-dinner entertainment made strenuous demands on the royal energies. There was a celebrated occasion when she and two friends dressed as Greek goddesses, retired to a boudoir and stripped before the King, who 'was ravished by the sight and examined every part about them with his own hands and eyes' as though they were a trio of nude statues and he a connoisseur of the beaux arts. The French have always been so much more imaginative than us about cabaret turns, but Louise simply didn't understand that it wasn't the best thing for the poor man's constitution. Next morning he had Parliament to contend with, to say nothing of the Bishops and quite a lot of arduous paperwork that went along with being Head of the Church of England.

This was where Nell's sheer professionalism came in. She had learned her whoring in the hard school at Madame Ross's élite brothel, patronised not just by the likes of Pepys and the Earl of Rochester, but by city merchants. The girls cost half a crown and learned to understand the needs of men with work to do next day. In the hot summer of 1675, when a party given for a German princeling in the Queen's apartments became too stuffy, it was Nell who proposed an adjournment to St James's Park. She took one look at the men sweating in their long wigs and the ladies fainting away in their stays and pointed out that the whole lot of them would be better off for some fresh air. Lords, ladies, musicians, waiters, bar and buffet set off immediately and when everyone felt better the entire court embarked, again at Nell's suggestion, for Hampton Court and sailed up the Thames to have breakfast there.

It was sound common sense like this which earned Nelly a reputation for having the King's true interests at heart, and caused the Londoners to take a very dim view of the sophisticated Louise. When Charles issued a Royal Proclamation shutting the coffee houses on the grounds that they attracted idlers and gossips, most people thought he had been put up to it by Louise. Pictures of her apartments were circulated with a caption in the inimitable style of the Earl of Rochester,

Within this place a bed's appointed
For a French bitch and God's anointed.

Charles eased his conscience on this score very elegantly. As King of England it was his duty to listen to foreign intelligence and since Louise was a French spy, sent to him expressly by Louis XIV, he regarded it as his political duty to sleep with her. It scandalised the Londoners, who emphasised Nell's virtue by calling her the Church of England whore. She was a regular parishioner at St Martin in the Fields and is buried in its crypt. The house in Pall Mall, where she and Charles gave birthday parties on Christmas Day for their son, the Duke of St Albans, is now the site of the Reform Club.

The French influence, however, left its mark in Restoration London in that a new refinement was introduced into the brothels. The old English bawdy houses, which had flourished up to the reign of Charles I, had resident staff, who doubled conveniently as bar maids, chamber maids and 'scrubbers'. This ensured a minimum of hygiene, but the new 'bagnios' built after the Great Fire and mostly in the Covent Garden area were luxuriously appointed and kept lists of professional beauties, so that the customers could study them at their leisure and then send for their choice. It was really like the distinction between set menus, and fine dishes selected from the à la carte. Molly King, Mother Douglas and Mrs Gould kept the best establishments, though Charles II preferred to roam about incognito and was a frequent patron of Madame Ross, where Nell served her apprenticeship. By the eighteenth century the lists had become scandalously mixed up and the names of society beauties and bona fide members of the acting profession sometimes appeared by mistake. Peg Woffington, Garrick's mistress, appeared on one and in another, which emphasised the charms of Irish ladies, there appears the name of that very Miss Gunning, who so steadfastly refused the attentions of the Duke of Hamilton until he married her.

This kind of thing did no good. A Mrs Goadby brought back brothels of the French kind with resident girls in the 1750s. The scene moved to Soho and has remained there ever since, but you will be pleased to learn, dear Reader, that there was no racial discrimination. A most respected black lady called Miss Harriett kept an establishment in Pall Mall. Mayfair at this point was renowned for its discretion and the trade was mostly carried on through hat shops, the millinery providing a front. The French connection which had begun in the days of Louise de Keroualle, was greatly enhanced just before the Revolution by the importation of Louis Quinze sofas, where unbuttoning could take place. This of course, put the whole business on a new footing. Hat shops went in for Louis Quinze sofas, which proliferated even in the reign of Louis XVI, when they had gone out of fashion. Then, after the Battle of Waterloo, when the returning officers were lionised throughout London, a Mrs Mary Wilson opened up a very fine brothel in Bond Street. She wrote books on the subject and translated Aretino, the Italian poet, who composed licentious satires.

Amid the general moral laxity of the Regency, the trade got rather out of hand. Some estimates say that in the early nineteenth century there were 5,000 brothels operating in London. Various regulations were brought in, but it is too painful to think of poor, dear Queen Victoria sullying her pure mind by giving the Royal Assent to such matters, when they became Acts of Parliament, so we will pass over them. In 1885 brothels were prohibited and in 1886 Mrs Josephine Butler, a great campaigner for women, put an end to compulsory medical examinations. She meant well, but the combination misfired, driving young women out on to the streets. In Edwardian England the streets were considered very unsafe for both sexes. Loitering went on all over Piccadilly. When Consuelo Vanderbilt, the young Duchess of Marlborough, paid her first call on Lady Lansdowne, she gathered that 'An English lady was hedged round with what seemed to be boring restrictions. One should not walk alone in Piccadilly, or in Bond Street, nor sit in Hyde Park unless accompanied. One should not be seen in a hansom cab and it was better to occupy a box than a stall at the theatre; to visit a music hall was out of the question.'

As the twentieth century progressed, the streets got worse. Things reached a dire pitch during the Second World War and I am sorry to say that the presence of the American Forces in Grosvenor Square did nothing to improve the situation. Nylon stockings, unobtainable in Britain even with clothing coupons, became an acceptable form of currency. So did fur coats and lipsticks by Max Factor. The era of the starlet had begun.

The shooting of a call girl in Park Street in 1958 led a national newspaper to call for a clean-up campaign. This brought about the 1959 Street Offences Act. The residents of Mayfair heaved sighs of relief, but the price of property escalated as call girls began to look for flats and bed-sitters near their old pitch of Curzon Street and Park Lane. Snobbery was rife with an apartment in Hill Street the ultimate goal. When Hugh Hefner opened his Playboy Club, with the bunny girls in their skin-tight satin costumes, a nude centrefold in *Playboy* also became a handy form of advertising. 'Hefner only employed nice girls,' said one ex-bunny who now owns a penthouse in Manhattan and a healthy chunk of Hampshire. 'We *were* nice girls, but after you'd done a centrespread, the temptations to go global were terrific. Hugh brought a new dimension to business entertaining. Then the Arabs struck oil. Who wanted to stay nice?'

Advertising is the perennial problem in Mayfair. The current system, which has made London telephone boxes the eighth wonder of the world, works like this. Early in the morning an advertising executive on a bicycle starts out with a supply of business cards, each bearing a picture, a telephone number and a list of special enticements. The usual route is from Goodge Street, up Oxford Street with a detour into Soho, a quick lunch near Marble Arch, followed by Park Lane, Shepherd Market, Berkeley Square, then off to Chelsea. Each telephone box on his route is lovingly decorated with cards offering hotel visits Special VIP Service, Specialist Striptease, or simple invitations to 'Live out your fantasies'. Most of the pictures are an outrage to public decency and various members of the two residents' associations fulminate accordingly. BT then send their own representative who takes all the cards down. Hot on the heels of the BT man comes another 'hookers' rep', who puts up a fresh lot of cards. This happens three times a day in most parts of London, but eight or nine times a day in Paddington. It is a uniquely British system, which puzzles foreigners, but it keeps everyone happy and ensures a great deal of paid employment. The first young man enjoys the artistry. From telephone boxes nicely done, it is a small step to the magic art of window dressing. The second young man enjoys a sense of moral outrage; he might eventually become a curate or a parking warden. The caller who arrives when the box has been cleaned up has a feeling 'that something is being done', and the card man who puts up the second or third lot enjoys a sense of compassion. He is, after all, looking after the needs of the poor helpless girls, who are so victimised by BT, that dangerous organisation which lures us all to spend money with the slogan, 'It's good to talk.'

In case anyone thinks that the Met are treating a serious problem with levity, Inspector Ward should have the last word in this chapter. He is the officer in charge of the Street Offences and Juvenile Protection Unit and the man who does most to restrain vice in Central London. Strenuous efforts are made to curb prostitution, but in a city as lively as ours, they do not always have the effect intended. Take the late seventies when the Met, backed by the Residents and Westminster Council, decided to clean up Shepherd Market. So many street-walkers were offending under Section 1/1 of the Act, which forbids loitering or soliciting in a public place, that a special squad of WPCs was sent in. A situation developed which can only be described as the reverse of kerb-crawling. The girls got into cars and pursued their regular clients, who hung about Shepherd Market waiting to be picked up. The business cards left in the phone boxes are usually carefully worded to remain within the limits of the Obscene Publications Act. 'You can't prosecute anyone,' Inspector Ward points out, 'for using the fine old electrical term ACDC. An offence called 'outraging public decency' is tryable only at the Central Criminal Court, so in Westminster a formal warning is the usual procedure.'

One offender, who was charged with kerb-crawling, pleaded guilty and appeared at Westminster Magistrates' Court. Halfway through the case the Judge asked him to change the plea to 'Not Guilty'. The defendant was adamant. It had been a fair cop and he wished to be fined or reprimanded. He wanted to break himself of the habit, he was, he said, 'Guilty'. At this point the Prosecution leaned forward and gently explained the reason the Vice Squad wanted the change. The lady of the night, whom the penitent kerb crawler had approached, had turned out to be a man.

11
Money

The reason the call girls covet a Hill Street address is that the cream stuccoed thoroughfare between Berkeley Square and South Audley Street has recently become renowned as a centre for Private Banking. Private banking is not to be confused with Merchant Banking. Merchant bankers take care of corporate requirements. They raise large sums of money for already-successful businesses to spend and they take up huge areas of Car Park 1 A in Ascot Week. Private bankers cater for individual needs. They deal with Serious Money and their top executives look deeply thoughtful all through Ascot Week. If you ever miss the Fourth Race on Gold Cup Day, because you are stuck in the tea queue behind a man who is deliberating between a smoked salmon sandwich and a prawn roll, you can be absolutely certain that he is a private banker. They have no sense of urgency.

Most of the customers at private banks are HNWIs, which is yet another inscrutable Americanism. The initials stand for High Net Worth Individual, which explains why the call girls value Hill Street and its environs. Quite a few members of the oldest profession have now gone corporate. Some are even richer than their original clients. They find it convenient to run off-shore tax syndicates, so naturally, they like to have friendly neighbours, who can help them to manage their assets. All private banks specialise in Asset Management. It works like this. If a rich person of any race, creed or colour goes to a private bank with a surplus, the asset manager says 'Buy a yacht'. Any fool can see why a yacht takes care of a surplus. A boat by defi-nition is a piece of wood/metal/fibreglass which you throw in the water and into which you then pour huge quantities of money. If the HNWI does not like sailing the private banker says, 'Buy a race horse', or if the HNWI is very rich indeed, 'Buy a racing stable'. The inference is that the expenses will be infinite and will mop up any surplus for years to come. Should the HNWI suffer from sea-sickness and an allergy to horseflesh, the private banker says, 'Buy some works of Art'. This last injunction does not mop up the surplus as swiftly and surely as the preceding two, but it helps to keep the British economy healthy.

Ideally the work of Art must be purchased in Mayfair, which means from Sotheby's, Mallett's, Agnew's or the Omell Galleries, but if the desired painting is not on sale there, then ten to one it will have found its way to the hinterland of St James's and can be purchased at Christie's, Spink's, Hazlitt Gooden and Fox, or N.R. Omell, who specialise in marine pictures and generously support the Royal National Lifeboat Institution. For the benefit of the landlocked classes we should explain that the RNLI is truly Cool Britannia. Its gallant crews provide off-shore rescue services along the coasts of the United Kingdom and the Republic of Ireland.

Once the HNWI has purchased his work of Art, it must be insured and hung – preferably in a room which is kept at a special temperature to ensure perfect conservation. It can then be admired by friends and visitors, examined by experts, mentioned in the *Burlington Magazine* and if the owner gives gracious permission, reproduced in several thousand art books, which will find their way on to coffee tables and into guest bedrooms all over the world. This means the owner has gone global. He is assured of a place in posterity and can be photographed by *Hello!* sitting on a Louis Quinze sofa smiling to camera with his face turned away from the work of Art, which hangs negligently in the background. He will immediately become the target of picture restorers, gallery owners and art thieves, who will all keep his name, address, ex-directory telephone number and e-mail details on a hit list.

The most famous art theft in Mayfair was when Georgiana, Duchess of Devonshire, was stolen from Agnew's. Sir William Agnew, son of the founder, Sir Thomas, bought Gainsborough's portrait of Georgiana wearing a large picture hat for 11,000 guineas at Christie's in 1876. The picture was exhibited at Agnew's, and one afternoon a thief called Adam Wirth cut the canvas from its frame, rolled it up and passed it out through a window to two accomplices waiting in the street. The thieves could not sell such a well-known picture, but they tried to extract a ransom from Sir William, by threatening to destroy it if he did not pay up. The case attracted a great deal of public interest and to prove they had the picture, the thieves kept cutting off bits of the canvas and posting them to Agnew's. Twenty-five years went by and Sir William refused to co-operate. Then in 1901 the last surviving member of the gang asked Pinkerton's, a Chicago detective agency, to act as go-between.

By now Sir William had retired, but his son, Morland Agnew, went to Chicago where the picture was restored to him. The two parties never met. Pinkerton's hired a suite in a Chicago hotel. The detectives sat with the picture in the middle room and the astonishing 'sale' was transacted between Morland Agnew in one ante-chamber and the thief in another. It is thought that the price paid to retrieve the picture was very small. The canvas was taken back to London and sold to the American millionaire, John Pierepont Morgan, who eventually gave it to the Metropolitan Museum, New York.

American money has always circulated very freely in London. When the War of Independence was in its bloodiest phase, George Washington was horribly inconvenienced by ill-fitting footwear. Before the War he had always bought his shoes and boots from a Mr Didsbury of Pall Mall, whose fame had spread through the gentlemen's clubs, so that he had patrons all over town. Like all good shoemakers, Mr Didsbury kept exact measurements of his customers' arches and insteps. When the War interrupted trade, George Washington had to buy American shoes. They obviously pinched, but the great leader, who was soon to become the first President of the United States bore it stoically. As soon as the Treaty of Paris was signed, however, George Washington unpatriotically gave up American boots and went straight back to Mr Didsbury. It shows that quality counts.

Americans have a different attitude towards money from us. They love to be lavish with the stuff and their generous attitude to spending sometimes makes our old-fashioned British reserve look like parsimony. American money on a grand scale poured into London in the 1890s, when the favourite status symbol for a Victorian beauty was to be painted by Sargeant. He charged 1,000 guineas a portrait. The Prince of Wales naively estimated the American painter's income at £10,000. Told it was nearer twice that, the heir to the Empire said wistfully, 'I wish I had £20,000 a year.' It followed that when he became Edward VII he encouraged foreign bankers to live in Mayfair and saw to it that his subjects stopped being nasty to the Jews. Elected an RA in 1897, Sargeant painted his enchanting study of the Wyndham Sisters the following year – Mrs Tennant, Mrs Adeane and Lady Elcho, soft, dovelike Victorian women. The Prince called the picture 'The Three Graces' and Sargeant's future income was assured.

Art sales boomed in the 1890s. Sargeant grew friendly with Mr Asher Wertheimer, the Bond Street dealer, who lived in Connaught Place in one of the new mansions in the rococo style – made fashionable by the Rothschilds with their palatial stronghold at the Piccadilly end of Park Lane. Eyebrows were raised at the Royal Academy however, when the American painter, who had once shocked Paris by his daring study of Madame Gautier with a slipped shoulder strap, exhibited a portrait of Wertheimer in all his Semitic shrewdness. It was a change from strong-chinned Englishmen. The old gentleman was delighted and a stream of Wertheimer portraits followed, including the picture of Ena and Betty, the sisters on the cover of this book. Painted in 1901 the portrait foreshadowed the bold role women would play in the new century. Sargeant knew Dame Ethel Smyth, the opera composer, who open admitted to being a Suffragette.

The Marlboroughs commissioned Sargeant in 1905. The Duke wished to have a companion piece to the great portrait Reynolds had painted of the fourth Duke and his family. It was to hang in full state at Blenheim, the Duke in Garter robes and the beautiful Consuelo – not yet fully consumed by the fires of the Women's Rights movement – in black, her sleeves lined with rose-coloured satin. Half way through the commission, the painter grew so bored by the pomposity of the Garter robes, that he swept them off to his studio in Tite Street and flung them round Betty Wertheimer, capturing their intricacies while she burlesqued a louche position.

This was the time when transatlantic travel was at its most gracious. Romances bloomed on ocean liners and the American rich bought, or built, palaces in Park Lane. The great boom of the Edwardian era had begun, but when Gordon Selfridge built his mighty store in Oxford Street, he simply wished to bring the American concept of *shopping* to ordinary people. As the giant edifice went up it elicited much criticism. People said it looked too much like Buckingham Palace to be a shop. Selfridge used American advertising methods, which to him were a part of that pioneering spirit he had learned as a $10 a week salesman at Marshall Field in Chicago. He was out to prove big is beautiful and more is better. On the opening day, 15 March 1909, one thousand assistants stood ready to serve in a hundred departments. The place boasted nine passenger lifts. At 9 am a bugler sounded a fanfare from the first floor balcony. One newspaper wrote: 'A crusade has been started to force on London superfluous luxuries with which markets are already overstocked across the Atlantic and elsewhere.'

Selfridge's methods were considered un-English and even un-ethical. Nevertheless in the first week over a million people flocked to the store and the great temple of consumerism has now flourished for nearly a century. To counter public disdain Selfridge was always very correctly dressed in a frock coat and a silk hat, but the pioneering spirit persisted under his gentlemanly exterior. He was a natural exhibitionist. When Blériot crossed the Channel three months after the store's grand opening, his aeroplane was put on show there. It promptly attracted a crowd of 150,000 – all potential customers. Some people say the Chicago tycoon had a mother fixation, when old Mrs Selfridge died, however, his love life blossomed. He rented Lansdowne House at the other end of Mayfair for £5,000 a year and from 1921 to 1929, it was the home of his protégées, the musical comedy artistes known as the Dolly Sisters. This was the period of the post-war slump. Devonshire House was sold in 1919 for over a million pounds, and four years later the fine old building was demolished to make way for a twelve-storey block in Portland stone. The Londoners were deeply shocked, since Devonshire House had been a landmark in Piccadilly for as long as anyone could remember. The great gates were placed ornamentally on the edge of Green Park and still bear the Cavendish motto, *Cavendo tutus*, Proceed With Caution. To passengers grid-locked in the traffic on a No 9 bus this injunction, visible through the window, seems like superfluous advice.

With the instinct of his breed the ninth Duke replenished his bank account and moved to smaller premises in Carlton Gardens. Horrified by the fate of his neighbour, Lord Lansdowne hung on until 1920. In its heyday Lansdowne House could hold more people than any other private residence in London. For political soirées the Grand Gallery, which was 100 feet long, was thrown open so that guests could admire the antique statuary and the wonderful paintings. The last great private party held there was the wedding reception for Lady Dorothy Cavendish and Harold Macmillan. The bride's parents, having so recently disposed of their own home, were busy trying to accommodate the Devonshire House art collection in their *bijou* mansion, so the bride's grandfather hosted the gathering, which was attended by swarms of aristocratic guests and headed by Queen Alexandra. The Macmillans countered with stars from the publishing world, inviting their top men of letters, including the venerable novelist Thomas Hardy. Lord Lansdowne recouped the cost of the wedding from Selfridge's rent.

Say what you like about the Dolly Sisters in their sequinned costumes and feathered head-dresses, they did keep money in constant circulation right through the roaring twenties. Hungarian showgirls, out for a good time, they filled Lansdowne House with guests who danced the Black Bottom and the Charleston until dawn. They had shingled hair. They wore revealing costumes on stage and they glittered with diamonds off it. Gloria Vanderbilt and Thelma, Lady Furness, once spotted Jenny Dolly in the casino at Cannes wearing emer-ald bracelets which reached to her elbows and with an emerald 'as big as an ice cube' in a ring on her left hand. Rosie Dolly said Selfridge asked her sister to marry him, but Jenny preferred to remain his mistress. The girls had taste. They got Selfridge to buy them a Hispano-Suiza, that most aristocratic of vehicles, but they were inclined to over indulge. Jenny loved ice-cream and when appearing in cabaret in Paris, she had whole planeloads of it flown over from Selfridge's food department daily. Whatever their moral values, the Dollys helped to keep Berkeley Square architecturally intact for a further decade. It was only after their departure that the Marquis caved in for the sum of £750,000. He sold Lansdowne House to facilitate the planned extension of Curzon Street into Berkeley Square. The eccentric siting of Adam's masterpiece obstructed the scheme. Relentlessly, in the name of thirties modernism, the two low graceful wings were shorn off and extra storeys were added behind a re-built façade.

In our own enlightened times English Heritage would never allow such a thing. You can imagine, dear Reader, the outcry. Even in the thirties, when the trees and gardens were considered expendable, there was an uproar. Two whole wings by Robert Adam simply lopped off! Once again American money came to the rescue. The First Drawing Room, painted soft duck egg blue and complete with decorations by Cipriani, Zucchi and Perfetti, was shipped to the Pennsylvania Museum of Art in Philadelphia. The Eating Room (*sic* in Adam's original plan and not Dining Room as it is often written) went to the Metropolitan Museum of Art in New York. The Met were particularly pleased, because the Eating Room included some of the First Marquis's collection of classical statuary, which has been nicely retained in the niches. The shorn stump of Lansdowne House became the Lansdowne Club. It was founded as the Bruton Club, a place for parents and their young to enjoy life together, but with the change of premises became the Lansdowne. Clubmen of the old school dismiss it as a 'cock and hen club' and its vast country membership includes many Anglican clergymen, among them the Rev Rex Hancock, who must be the last hunting parson in England. Many members are married couples. Jean-Pierre, the present club steward, swears he can spot illicit lovers hoping to misuse the bedrooms a mile off. When the club first opened it was expected that in the style of the 1930s there would be dancing every night. A Sun Loggia was built at the top, decorated with a lewd mural, caricaturing social and political figures of the day. Cognoscenti of the era are still arguing about the shape and *placement* of Lady Diana Cooper's breasts on a reclining figure in Egyptian undress. The Club remained open throughout the Second World War, when the squash courts were turned in emergency dormitories. Exhausted lady members, who had been driving for the MTC (Motorized Transport Corps) remember gratefully flopping onto mattresses laid side by side on the floor, but, 'to distinguish it from a school dorm, with the sheets turned down as though you were staying at the Ritz.' MI5 the Secret Service building was next door. Richard Arnold-Baker recalls travelling across occupied France with Sir Frank Nelson, the chief of Britain's sabotage operation. They drove a Morris 8 and held up petrol stations with a revolver. Just after Dunkirk they boarded a troop ship which hadn't been sunk and landed at Milford Haven. When Richard reached Berkeley Square in clothes he had worn for fourteen consecutive days, the Lansdowne Porter said 'Good afternoon, Sir. We thought you was dead,' and sent a bottle of champagne to his room.

Nowadays the Club is a great centre of Scottish dancing. The Ballroom is graced by the De Laslo portrait of the Queen Mother, as Duchess of York. She was a great one for Eightsomes in her youth. 'We do an awful lot of reeling at the Lansdowne' said a kilted member of the Under thirty-fives. Because of its size the club absorbed, or housed, other establishments, when they ran into difficulties, or leases expired. It sheltered the Portland, the world's most authoritative bridge club, the Royal Aero Club and the colourful Savages who sang loudly on Friday evenings. They have since moved to the National Liberal Club, which has sound-proofing. The Wine and Food Society had headquarters at the Lansdowne until recently and in 1969 the International Sportsmen's Club went under the hospitable roof. With a swimming pool in the basement the club has always had an athletic bias. It is internationally famous for fencing and squash. Americans are keen to join the Lansdowne, or to visit the spot where the historic Treaty was signed, which has led to some smartening of the bedrooms and modernisation of the plumbing. The thirties décor has been swept away in favour of Adam's original design, grandly restored. The gilders who did the Crush Hall were also responsible for the Queen's new ceilings at Windsor Castle. All this has brought in a rash of complaints from country members who fear the subscriptions will go up. With the proliferation of international banking in the area, their fears may be justified, but under the re-gilded ceilings the rules of clubland still apply. If brash new members try to open up briefcases in the public rooms, they will be courteously reproved. To be sure to maintain balance on such a ticklish subject, I asked a Lansdowne member who has lived all his grown up life in Upper Brook Street, where the dividing line between Old and New money lay. Without batting an eyelid he replied that 'New Money is anything after the South Sea Bubble.'

Citibank the New York company was the first 'merchant venturer' to establish a *private* bank in Hill Street, at 41 Berkeley Square. Mrs Elizabeth Forsyth a lady with a talent for money-making was one of its employees. She moved across Hill Street to join Asil Nadir, the Cypriot newspaper owner, who bought up Thorn Electrical and Del Monte, the orange juice people. His Polly Peck empire was based at 42 Berkeley Square. At first everyone was happy, especially the British housewife, delighted by the prospect of cheap steam irons and life-restoring Vitamin C. Unfortunately the Serious Fraud Squad raided No 42 and accused Mr Nadir of Insider Dealing. Mrs Forsyth did ten months in Holloway Prison for handling money alleged to have been stolen by Mr Nadir, but Mr Nadir was never found guilty of theft. The story has a happy ending because Mrs Forsyth won her appeal and is again a respected consultant in international finance, though she speaks darkly of the cuisine in Holloway Prison.

As the private banks proliferated the old Polly Peck premises were acquired by Pasley-Tyler & Co, and turned into the newest and most original of London clubs. Robert Pasley-Tyler dreamed up the idea of turning the magnificent period house, which Mr Nadir had renovated into a haven of luxurious office suites, but with the atmosphere of a pleasant country house.

Now that the great days of ocean travel are over, nothing is more stressful for the busy executive than crossing the Atlantic. He can fly by the most exclusive airline in the world, but once he reaches Heathrow, he is subject to exactly the same pressures as we who go Virgin Atlantic. His Louis Vuitton luggage can get lost in transit. He may be swooped on by an over-zealous customs official who will leaf through every single page of his new Bill Bryson – and his copy of *Who Owns Whom* under the impression that he has concealed a milligram of cocaine there. He has probably already been delayed by some challenge over air-space, which has kept his plane circling above Middlesex for half an hour, and he will be whisked along the M25 to get grid-locked on the M4. Undoubtedly there will be road works near the Chiswick flyover and a tail-back at Hammersmith. When his limousine finally penetrates Piccadilly, his mobile phone needs re-charging from over use as he deftly switches appointments and re-programmes the next twenty four hours of his life. As the limo circles Berkeley Square he is almost certainly practising his wife's yoga breathing exercises to stay sane. He then steps into the deeply relaxing atmosphere of Pasley-Tyler House and sinks into one of the red-chequered sofas. His cares may be global, his second wife suing for an unreasonable divorce, and his daughter's pre-nuptial with a man she met last summer at Martha's Vineyard may be preying on his mind, but suddenly at his elbow there is David.

This genius among dining room managers anticipates his innermost wish. Be it a Bloody Mary or a packet of Nurofen, David produces it with the air of one who has ministered to Real Gentlemen all his life. He glides behind the bar, which is actually the teller's kiosk from an old French bank. A slightly worn Turkish rug completes the effect. If the executives' deals go smoothly he can purchase the paintings from local auction houses, which adorn the walls. The prices are not extortionate. I was shown a huge Van Dyke going for a mere one point eight million – dollars, not pounds. Serious Money is the order of the day, but in the country house atmosphere of Pasley-Tyler the executive feels there is no cause for panic. The Signing Room used by grandees from BP has optional computers concealed in mahogany cabinets, while another suite is dominated by a wedding picture of George Villiers, Duke of Buckingham and Lady Katherine Manners, represented as Venus and Adonis.

She is coyly robed from the waist down, but displays her softly rounded assets, while he is handsomely naked, except for a brief hunting tunic, covering the appropriate parts. The figures are eight feet high. Despite her classically bared breasts,

Lady Katherine is wearing her pearls. We Europeans, with our quaint distinctions between Old and New money, do know how to live.

12
Shopping to Survive

To those who remember Atkinson's lavender water and baby linen bought for a King's ransom from the White House, Bond Street will always be the most quintessentially English of streets. To the young it means Gucci and DKNY, and thus symbolises Power Dressing at a globally recognisable level. However, Bond Street in the eighteenth century was no place for ladies. On the site now occupied by Asprey's, where the road narrows into the 'Bond Street Straits', stood the Clarendon Hotel, which stretched back into Albemarle Street. Nearby Stephen's Hotel was much frequented by army officers, who used it like a private club. On summer evenings they sat outside smoking long clay pipes in their shirt sleeves. Bachelors lodged in the area and the shops supplied gentlemen's needs. Tailors, hatters, wig-makers and barbers opened premises, but there were no milliners, dressmakers, or ladies' hairdressers.

Very soon the street was known as a 'lounge', a place where the bucks and the beaux met to parade new fashions. One shirt-maker offered lessons in tying cravats, a fad which the Regency dandies, Beau Brumell and Count D'Orsay would eventually raise to an Art Form. If ladies ventured into this exclusive male preserve in their carriages or sedans, they risked being ogled by 'the Bond Street loungers', idle young men about town satirised in plays of the time for affecting a special walk known as 'the Bond Street roll'. One vile cartoon called 'Peepers in Bond Street' shows fashionable ladies wearing the newest plumed head-dresses introduced by Georgiana Duchess of Devonshire, lifting up their skirts to get into carriages without dirtying the hems of their gowns. The men crouch lecherously in the gutter, using their spy glasses to peep up the ladies' skirts at their legs and garters.

Old Bond Street dates back to 1686. Sir Thomas Bond, after whom it was named, died bankrupt, as did most members of the consortium who built it. They were property speculators, who bought the Duke of Albemarle's house in 1683. They pulled it down and planned four new streets – Albemarle Street, Dover Street, Stratton Street and Bond Street on the site. Evelyn snobbishly described them as 'certain inferior people, rich bankers and merchants', for the gulf between trade and Society was quite unbridgeable. New Bond Street was not developed until 1721, and when the comparatively modest houses went up enterprising tradesmen seized eagerly upon them as handy for Hanover Square, where the rich Whig puritans were building.

This made it easier for the merchants to show their wares, for in the eighteenth century much shopping was done from home. Tradesmen brought samples or lists of supplies to the houses of the nobility and gentry. They sat in the hall on hard-backed chairs, until the lord or lady of the house was ready to receive them. They were not, of course, permitted to use the front doors of great houses, but went in by the tradesmen's entrance. From the start there was an impregnable social barrier between Old Bond Street and New Bond Street. Few spoke of it, but everyone was aware that it existed. In Old Bond Street aristocratic transactions went on. The shopkeepers were not tradespeople, but connoisseurs, dealers in fine art and luxury goods. In New Bond Street shops opened to supply life's necessities, fish, writing paper and wig powder. Servants were sent to make such purchases and the snobbery between old and new has lasted almost to the present day. My mother swept me into Fenwick's when I was eighteen to equip me with my first 'little black dress'. It was silk grosgrain, a designer piece by today's standards. Having approved the fit, Mother, a shopper of the old school, severely advised me to 'wear it as though it came from Fortnum's or Simpson's of Piccadilly'. She knew Mayfair like the back of her hand and considered it a sign of having gone down in the world to shop in *New* Bond Street.

In addition to the specialist shops, itinerant vendors patrolled the streets of Mayfair crying their wares. A famous series of prints was put out by Ackermann commemorating old London street cries. 'Cherry ripe' was the call in summer, when girls with baskets came to Town from the Kentish orchards, or from the market gardens of Chelsea. Muffins and lavender were sold this way right up to the 1950s, but today the only survivors of the old tradition are chestnut sellers, who place their braziers outside museums and art galleries, and French onion men, who mostly confine themselves to Fulham and Chelsea. I have never seen a French onion man pedalling down Piccadilly, but I once arbitrated in an Anglo–Gallic dispute, when a Westminster park-ing warden tried to prevent an onion seller from chaining his bicycle to some railings near the London Library. Violence threatened to erupt and, being reasonably proficient in both languages, I offered my services as an interpreter. It turned out that the Frenchman wished to use the gentleman's lavatory at Fortnum and Mason. I cannot remember what happened to the warden but I grandly ushered the onion man into the Cavendish Hotel, where the top-hatted doorman minded the bike. After he had spent his penny, the onion man treated me to fine French cognac in the Sub-Rosa Bar. It was a gesture of which Rose Lewis, the Duchess of Jermyn Street, would have approved.

Rosa was Edward VII's favourite cook. She learned her art in the household of the Comte de Paris, the exiled heir to the French throne. Wherever she found herself, Rosa insisted on shopping personally for fresh produce every morning. Her menus, whether for the English nobility or the wildly assorted guests at the Cavendish, the raffish hotel in Jermyn Street, which made her a legend, were always in perfect French. On this score she made no concessions, not even in 1907, when on the King's recommendation she was engaged to cook for Kaiser Wilhelm II, who was on summer vacation at Highcliffe Castle. The Kaiser hated all things French with the exception only of champagne. At table he patriotically served German hocks and Bavarian beer. He brought a retinue of ninety people to Highcliffe and the village shops soon ran out of stores. Rosa travelled daily between London and Kent to buy her vegetables from Covent Garden and her groceries from Jackson's of Piccadilly, commandeering a Special Train for the purpose.

. . . a Westminster parking warden tried to prevent an onion seller from chaining his bicycle to some railings . . .

During his stay several prominent London hostesses, including Princess Daisy of Pless, the Duchess of Westminster and Lady Randolph Churchill, entertained the Kaiser. They all called upon Rosa to cook freelance. When she went to cook in country houses, she usually upset the resident staff by her vigorous swearing and her extravagant use of cream, but she was invariably beautifully dressed and in her fine white blouses full of tucks and pleats, and long tailored skirts, was frequently mistaken for a society lady. On one occasion in the house of Mrs Harry McCalmont, the Marchioness of Bath's grandmother, the King seeing Rosa sampling the champagne, kissed her. When the guests were ready to go in to dinner, Edward VII commented on the absence of the beautiful lady he had met earlier. 'That,' said his hostess, 'must have been Mrs Lewis, the cook.' 'I gave her a kiss,' said the King. 'In that case,' replied Mrs McCalmont, 'we shall certainly have an excellent dinner.'

Before the First World War, when the Cavendish was in its heyday, the hotel boasted one of the finest cellars in London. Copious quantities of champagne were consumed every evening. A latter day Robin Hood, Rosa robbed the rich to supply 'the poor'. Young men she approved of, or whose fathers she knew, would be charged very little and their drinks would be put on the accounts of those whom she considered too rich, or too mean with their money. When War was declared she banished her signed photo of the Kaiser to a downstairs loo. As part of her War Effort, she would accept cheques from young officers on leave. If they had endured the horrors of the trenches she would stuff the cheques in a drawer, uncashed. Despite food rationing, she made daily forays into Fortnum's for plovers' eggs and foie gras, which she served indiscriminately to Lloyd George and Mr Asquith, or young men who had come home on leave.

Sometimes Rosa would drive to Victoria Station in her Daimler and pick up a carload of soldiers, who had nowhere to spend the night. She would provide every comfort from hot baths to 'a nice clean tart', for Rosa knew everyone in Piccadilly and everyone knew Rosa. Lord Ribblesdale, who had been Lord in Waiting to Queen Victoria, was her most distinguished guest. He went to live at the Cavendish after the death of his beloved wife, Charty, the sister of Margot Asquith. Tall, handsome and patrician, his portrait by Sargent hangs in the Tate and, in replica, above the staircase of the Cavendish. With such a glittering coterie of admirers Rosa was always received at the best parties, but her cavalier attitude to shopping never changed. At one of Gordon Selfridge's famous election parties in the thirties Rosa arrived with Lord Charles Cavendish. Entering the room together they gave one of the dessert trolleys a hearty push, so that it slithered across the floor, gathering momentum as it rolled across to where the Dolly Sisters were arranged in a cascade of feathers and diamonds. Rosa's exit was equally spectacular. She picked up a whole salmon she liked the look of, telling the waiter to 'Put it on my account at Fortnum and Mason's'.

Lord Ribblesdale's sister-in-law, Margot Tennant, did not, as a young girl, look as though she would have the makings of a great shopper. She was something of a tomboy and had been raised at Glen, a Scottish baronial property belonging to the Tennants on the borders of Peebleshire and Selkirk. When she arrived in London for her coming out, she bought a beautiful bay horse for herself at Tattersall's to ride in the Row. Waiting for her father to escort her one morning, she decided to ride into the hallway of 40, Grosvenor Square to give her parent a surprise. Without dismounting she rode her steed up the steps and across the polished floor, rather proud of her dressage skills and obviously enjoying showing off before the footmen. Unfortunately the noble animal caught a glimpse of himself in a mirror, reared violently, crashing his mistress's top hat into the chandelier, and slipped on the parquet. Down went everything: Margot, pony and chandelier. Both horse and rider were up in a moment, but thoroughly frightened by the unfamiliar scenario, the horse kicked a fine old English chest 'into a jelly'. When Miss Tennant eventually became Mrs Asquith, wife of the distinguished Liberal Prime Minister, her behaviour continued in this forceful vein.

Like most Prime Ministers' wives, she was determined to dress for the part. Margot was no ingenue. She already patronised Lucile, the great English dressmaker of the 1890s, who scandalised Victorian husbands by creating cobweb fine underwear, instead of robust petticoats of nun's veiling. Lucile was the sister of the novelist Elinor Glyn. She later married Sir Cosmo Duff Gordon and moved her couture business to Hanover Square. When Margot Asquith first went to her, Lucile was the first dressmaker to use live mannequins and to have a showroom in the modern sense. Her models paraded on an elegant grey stage backed by a soft grey curtain before an audience of rather avant-garde society women and a few celebrities such as Ellen Terry, Lily Langtry and the Duchess of Westminster. From dressing chez Lucile, Mrs Asquith graduated to Paris, where the most sensational designer of the decade was Paul Poirot. He remembered her entering his salon 'like a thunderclap', announcing how she wished to be dressed and showing him her velvet satin knickers. 'Monsieur Poirot,' she said, 'Englishwomen must know your dresses. They are dresses for aristocrats and great ladies.'

Margot proceeded to give a tea party at 10, Downing Street to which she asked her most elegant friends to view M. Poirot's creations. The press were scandalised. Ever since the 1830s when William IV's wife, Queen Adelaide, had banned French fashions from Court to encourage the home textile industry, the wives of British Prime Ministers had patronised English dressmakers. There were questions in Parliament. Mr Asquith was accused of facilitating the 'intrusion of foreign merchandise' by allowing his wife to organise 'exhibitions in the residence which has been paid for by the nation's trade'. Margot's great shopping days were over. Next time she was in Paris Paul Poirot reported, 'The poor woman no longer dared to meet me. She had to order dresses in London to give the shops proof of her loyalty and fidelity.'

In the heady days after the First World War, when the Charleston was the rage, American hostesses vied to storm London Society. In England the distinctions between Old and New money were very far from erased and merciless stories were told of Laura Corrigan, the Wisconsin girl, who worked as a waitress in Cleveland, Ohio. Laura married James Corrigan of the Corrigan–McKinney Steel Company. As a wedding present he gave her a $17,000 Rolls-Royce with a chauffer to drive it and a footman to open the door. It set a lifestyle which she was determined to keep up. Nevertheless Laura found it difficult to break into East Coast Society. As Mrs James Corrigan her dream was to give the kind of lavish parties with which Mrs Vanderbilt and Mrs Stuyvesant-Fish tried to outshine each other in New York. At one point the Corrigans were said to be worth sixty million dollars, but it did not buy Laura the *entrée* she dreamed of and when her husband died, she set her sights on London.

Her income was $800,000 a year. She rented No 16, Grosvenor Square and advertised her democratic views by instructing the butler that anyone who came to the door should be given a cocktail, regardless of whether it was the butcher's boy, or the Duke of York. Laura was a truly spontaneous shopper. Sometimes she would improvise a party by requisitioning the entire stock of Fortnum and Mason's grocery department. She also copied the Vanderbilt custom of lavishing little presents upon her guests: diamond-encrusted cigarette cases or gold sock suspenders for the men, powder compacts studded with jewels for the women. Cartier's adored her.

Wicked stories were told of her malapropisms. The Grosvenor Square house was rented from the Keppels. Mrs Keppel had been Edward VII's mistress in the era when he was nicknamed Prince Tum Tum. Mrs Keppel was also noticeably stout, so it was perhaps not inappropriate that Laura called 16, Grosvenor Square my little 'ventre à terre'. She once solemnly assured a caller that the Keppels' chairs were all covered in 'petit pois'. When asked to take care of the priceless Aubusson carpets, she replied 'Why? They're not even new.'

Laura rented different houses for each London Season. Most were in Mayfair. One year she took Crewe House in Curzon Street, now the Saudi Arabian Embassy. More famously she took Dudley House, 100, Park Lane, at the then staggering rent of £5,000 for two months. Among her true friends she numbered the Duke of Marlborough, whom she often partnered in a spectacular version of the Charleston, Lady Diana Cooper, who loved her brash and unpretentious common sense and Princess Marina of Greece, whom she had met in Paris, long before her marriage into the British royal family. When the Princess's engagement to the Duke of Kent was announced, Laura very practically took her shopping for a full-length mink coat to keep out the English winters. The Press vulgarly learned the price and Laura's enemies made spiteful jokes about her attempts to 'buy' her way into royal circles. Nothing could have been further from the truth. The Greek royal family were not wealthy and the Princess was delighted to have such a beautiful item as part of her trousseau. Only once did Mrs Corrigan receive a reprimand for her familiarity. The new Duchess of Kent won first prize in a charity tombola. Laura shouted 'Marina's won it. Marina's won it.' The following morning a palace equerry called. Nobody minded Mrs Corrigan's natural excitement, or that her voice had risen to a most unladylike pitch, but what she should have screamed was, 'Her Royal Highness has won it.'

Stories of the great hostess's spending habits could fill volumes, but Great Shoppers are not the same as Big Spenders. The psychology which led Sir Bernard and Lady Docker to drive a gold-plated Daimler, or Richard Burton to buy Elizabeth Taylor the biggest diamond in the world is a separate thing. Shopping is more of an art form; spending a kind of fever. One hostess famous between the Wars was Lady Cunard, widow of Sir Bache Cunard the shipping millionaire. Whole chapters have been written about Emerald Cunard's parties, about her skills as a hostess, her guests, her jewels, her tiny feet, her elegant ripostes and her friendship with Sir Thomas Beecham, but there are seldom any stories about her going shopping. When she did it was in that casual unhurried manner, so typical of those from the West Coast of America, for Emerald Cunard with all her European sophistication came originally from California. She never completely grasped the importance of punctuality in English Society and during the brief interval before the Abdication, arrived late for a dinner party at which she had been placed between her host, Chips Channon and the new King, Edward VIII. Such was her charm that when she finally swept in everyone forgave her.

No one ever scolded Emerald for her unpunctuality until Sir Thomas Beecham ostentatiously kept an orchestra and the whole audience waiting for her to turn up at a concert in Oxford. When she finally appeared, chattering away to Kenneth Clark, Sir Thomas turned to face the audtiorium and bellowed,

'You're late. Sit down.' The only other time she was reprimanded was by Lord d'Abernon. Arriving forty-five minutes
after a luncheon party had begun, she explained very sweetly
that she had been shopping. 'My dear, I was held up. I went to
buy a chandelier.' Lord d'Abernon was polite but firm. 'I once
had a friend,' he told her, 'who bought a chandelier after
lunch.'

13
Marriage in Mayfair

'Get me to the church on time' is a regular *cri de coeur* before Mayfair weddings now that the traffic is permanently grid-locked. The bridegroom who immortalised the song was Eliza Doolittle's father, and when Shaw unleashed the original version of *Pygmalion*, Alfred Doolittle was on his way to St George's Hanover Square.

In 1913 Shaw's cockney dustman, who becomes a capitalist toff and ties the nuptial knot in Society's favourite church, was a far-fetched caricature who kept West End audiences rocking with laughter. Nowadays when capitalist refuse executives are as common as billionaire footballers, or supermodels who don't get out of bed for under £10,000 a day, Alfred Doolittle's wedding wouldn't even rate a paragraph in the *Londoner's Diary*. In 1956, however, when Lerner and Loewe wrote *My Fair Lady*, 'I'm getting married in the morning' with its vigorous refrain was an immediate hit. The words and the tune made Alfred Doolittle a household name and the show played all over the world for decades. Possibly the original joke about St George's Hanover Square was lost on the first night audience, who flocked to Broadway to see Julie Andrews as Eliza and the inimitable Rex Harrison playing Professor Higgins. Almost certainly it was misunderstood in Moscow, but when the English version opened in Drury Lane, the joke had stood the test of time.

St George's is the parish church of Mayfair. From the outset it has been associated with the Good Things in Life. In 1711 Parliament provided for fifty new London churches to serve the capital's spiritual needs. St George's was to be financed, like St Paul's Cathedral, by a tax on coal. The residents of the half-built Hanover Square petitioned for a church of their own, as St

Martin's was still quite literally, if not '*in* the Fields', *across* them, and necessitated a muddy morning walk. Queen Anne's Commander in Chief in Ireland, General William Stuart, duly offered a plot of land adjoining Maddox Street and George Street and John James, who had been apprenticed to Wren and was a friend of Hawksmoor, was commissioned to design the church. By June 1721 General Stuart laid the foundation stone. He poured a libation of wine and in brisk military fashion instructed the Lord God of Heaven to 'preserve the Church of St George'.

The Almighty complied willingly. Resident in the parish by 1725 there were nine Dukes, two Marquesses, twenty-two Earls, six Viscounts, twelve Barons, with an Archbishop and a Bishop or two for good measure. The worshippers consisted of the chief nobility of England and the names of the Church Wardens, inscribed in gold lettering on the panels of the gallery read like a random sample from *Burke's* or *Debrett*. Everyone went to church, so that in the eighteenth century Morning Prayer was rather like a party at Devonshire House, only of course with more solemnity. With such aristocratic patrons, the church was able to commission the best craftsmen and artists to embellish the interior. William Kent painted a splendid Last Supper which hangs behind the altar, with the disciples on couches, cosily framed by the reredos. Above it a magnificent stained glass window represents the Tree of Jesse, which emphasises the kingly descent and general blue-bloodedness of the Saviour of Mankind, rather than any odd notions about carpentry and humility. Seven silver lamps proclaim the presence of the Holy Sacrament. The carpets are crimson, the pews polished mahogany, the kneeling cushions proper leather and the organ, which dominates the west wall, is surely the most majestic in England. Handel's advice was sought when it was installed as he lived nearby in Brook Street. The great composer instantly dashed off an extempore theme to test the pipes.

St George's dispenses a top brand of reassuringly no-nonsense High Anglicanism. The present incumbent, the Rev William Maynard Atkins, has been rector since 1955. At time of writing he is in his late eighties and delivers the Sunday sermon in a voice without a quaver. You do not get the impression that his congregation dashes about London breaking the seventh commandment and there is certainly no truck with Rites A and B. Just the good old 'Interim Rite' devised by Thomas Cranmer in 1549. There has never been a breath of scandal attached to the running of St George's, except for when the crypt was let out as a wine store, which shocked the Bishop of London in 1805. The preachers have been exemplary and just punishment was visited on the only man who tried to bribe his way into gaining the living. In 1774 Dr William Dodd, a royal chaplain, offered an inducement to the Lord Chancellor's wife to gain him the appointment. She reported the matter to Parliament and Dr Dodd was hanged at Tyburn. With such a grand reputation it is not surprising that St George's has always been a popular venue for Society weddings and the Parish Register is filled with the signatures of the great and the good.

Two royal Dukes married there and one royal Duke, Queen Victoria's wicked uncle, the Duke of Sussex married there twice. The first time he broke the Royal Marriage Act, but the second time he respected it. The Queen was so delighted to see him mend his ways that she created his new bride Duchess of Inverness. As the lady was the widow of the Lord Mayor of London and had previously been plain Mrs Buggins, the title must have been a welcome relief. A few decades earlier the Duke of Wellington was in great demand at St George's, both as a wedding witness and for the giving away of brides, in the outburst of marrying which followed Waterloo. In the year 1816, one thousand and sixty-three weddings were celebrated at St George's and the Iron Duke's signature occurs many times in the parish register. No doubt an enterprising historian will some day write a PhD thesis on Waterloo Weddings and the After Effects of Battle Euphoria. Were they pregnancy-related? Who were the conquerors and whom the conquered, at the many celebratory balls given to mark Boney's defeat? Did the young ladies of good family, who swooned in droves over the returning heroes, express their admiration with too much warmth in the rose arbour? Was it parental pressure or the demands of honour which forced certain gallant heroes into unions they spent a lifetime repenting? What was the influence of the all-revealing muslin dress, popularised by the *ci-dessus* Empress Josephine and, since the ending of the French War, available once more in London? 'Naked fashions,' as Jane Austen so scathingly put it, in which the belles tempted the beaux as they whirled about the Regency ballrooms to the intoxicating strains of the waltz.

One of the most sensational brides at St George's was the 'Spanish' dancer, Lola Montez, who married George Heald, a gallant young Life Guard there in 1849. Hanover Square was besieged by reporters. They swarmed around the portico to get a better view of the bride, who had almost brought down the government of Bavaria, after her tempestuous liaison with its ruler, King Ludwig I. She left the German principality on the verge of revolution and sought refuge in Half Moon Street. Rescued by her dashing new admirer, who by good luck had an income of £10,000 a year, she signed the register as the Countess of Landsfeld, a title conferred by the lovesick Ludwig. Unfortunately her first husband, whom she had presumed dead, resurrected himself and the couple were obliged to flee to Spain to avoid bigamy proceedings. When George Heald died, the Irish beauty (née Marie Dolores Gilbert) returned to the stage. She toured America and Australia with her Spanish dance troupe, but developed a distinct hostility to the Press and on one memorable occasion horse-whipped the editor of the *Ballarat Times.*

Shelley married at St George's, having earlier eloped with the sixteen-year-old Harriet Westbrook. They went through a form of marriage in Edinburgh, but after three years of nomadic existence decided to renew their vows in the Anglican Church. This was not a success. The marriage collapsed and two years later Harriet drowned herself in the Serpentine, leaving Shelley to set up his celebrated menage à trois with the fifteen-year-old Claire Clairmont and Mary Godwin, the author of *Frankenstein.* Another literary marriage was that of Mary Anne Evans, better known as the novelist, George Eliot. In 1880, when the bride was at the height of her fame, she married her financial adviser, John Cross. He was forty and she was sixty-one. She had had an earlier liaison with G.H. Lewes, a married man, which lasted until his death. When Mary Anne became Mrs Cross, she received a congratulatory note from her brother, Isaac, who had not spoken to her since 1857. Margot Tennant, inevitably, married her Mr Asquith at St George's. The witnesses were Lord Rosebery, Mr Balfour and Mr Gladstone, who were all at some time Prime Minister. With the inclusion of the bridegroom's own signature, the entry was endorsed by four Prime Ministers. Mr Gladstone gave the couple his seven volume work, *Gleanings*, as a wedding present. The bride was attended by ten bridesmaids and members of the public fought to gate crash the event. A gentleman with a gardenia in his buttonhole tried to bribe Margot's old nanny to sell him a ticket.

St George's continued to be the premier venue for Society weddings until the 1920s, when St Paul's Knightsbridge pushed it into second place. Fashionable Catholic Weddings are usually held at the Jesuit Church of the Immaculate Conception in Farm Street. The back door is in Mount Street and a handy covered way leads almost directly from the vestry to the Connaught Hotel. This is perfect for receptions, as the Head Chef of the Connaught is second to none. American heiresses of the better sort have been known to book in there when they have set their sights on gourmet members of the Peerage.

One such lady, on hearing the seventh Lord Sudeley was taking a course of Roman Catholic instruction, assumed he was intending to tie the nuptial knot. She proceeded to his bachelor apartment and requested to see the water-colours of his ancestral home. As many of these hung round his four poster, he rashly led her into his bedroom. He had just begun to explain the fenestration of Toddington, a subject close to his lordship's heart, when he noticed the lady had taken off all her clothes and got into his bed. Remembering that there was something he urgently needed to see at the Wallace Collection, Lord Sudeley made a diplomatic exit and left her to it. His great interest in the Roman Catholic Faith had been prompted by the fact that he was Lay-Patron of the Prayer Book Society, and wished to explore the beauties of rival liturgies.

Claridges also lies conveniently close to Farm Street and a good many receptions take place there. At the wedding of a well known Catholic doctor this was the arrangement: Mass first and a sit-down lunch in the French Salon after. The wedding day dawned. At least fifty per cent of the congregation were praying that the bridegroom would arrive on time, since his reputation for punctuality was not high. To everyone's surprise, the bride-groom was in place at least half an hour before the bride was due. Eyebrows were raised, bets exchanged as to the means employed by the Best Man to ensure such a miracle. The cele-brant was the late Father John Tracy, who coincidentally was the very priest who had instructed Lord Sudeley. Father Tracy was once a theatrical chaplain in Scotland. His absolution was strict, but his reputation for finding impediments second to none. If ever a hapless Catholic, as is sometimes the case, made an uncanonical marriage by mistake, Father Tracy S. J. was the man to undo it. He was a dab hand at weaving his way through the intricacies of ecclesiastical law, and if ever he found a loophole Father Tracy would come up with a Declaration of Freedom, to pave the way for a second and more permanent arrangement. As it happened the doctor did not need such a document. His earlier marriage had not been recognised by the Roman Church.

On his second wedding day the auspices were excellent. The weather seemed uncertain and the skies were leaden, but Father Tracy was in place. The Voluntary was played twice to cover the bride's lateness and after an expectant pause it was followed by a soothing rendition of 'Sheep may safely graze'. The bride-groom was displaying mild anxiety. The congregation rustled the Order of Service and over at Claridge's the sous-chef trans-ferred the canapés to a warmer. At last the bride arrived, but just as she entered the west door a thunderclap echoed through the heavens. The wedding, however, proceeded without a hitch and the joyful couple were driven to Claridge's followed by a proces-sion of elegant guests.

A glorious event took place. The French Salon was awash with pretty dresses and even prettier hats. Mr Edward Goodyear, the only court florist in London to boast *four* royal appoint-ments, had decorated the tables exquisitely. The company was stimulating and I was on my second glass of champagne, when Father Tracy appeared at my elbow.

'Phew,' he said. 'I never prayed so hard in all my life.'

'Oh Father, I'm so glad. They are such a well-matched couple.'

'No,' he said, 'not the wedding. The *wiring*.'

Farm Street at the time was in the midst of roof repairs and it transpired that at the very moment the bride had entered the church, a rivulet of water had run down the west wall inches from the main electricity cable. Only Father Tracy could see what was happening from his vantage point in the Sanctuary. Oblivious that a blackout threatened, the choir were sweetly singing 'Jubilate Deo' in the Orlando di Lasso version, as the little rivulet of moisture gathered momentum. The Nuptial Mass followed and the congregation then belted out 'Praise my soul the King of Heaven' with the enthusiasm customary to those focussing inwardly on the thought of luncheon at Claridge's. The little rivulet had by now turned into a steady stream, which was creeping along the wall. Fervently muttering, 'Please Lord, don't let the lights go out' Father Tracy concentrated hard on the signing of the register. Only when the congregation were genuflecting away, before filing out, did he begin to relax. The final voluntary at that wedding was by César Franck – 'Pièce Héroique'.

14
Charity Begins in Mayfair

'Thank you for your pennies. Thank you for your pennies,' the vibrant blonde pouring the coffee after High Mass at Farm Street is the Baroness Stefania von Kories zu Goetzen. Earrings flashing, she exhorts the faithful to pay up in the low period which traditionally follows the Christmas bonanza. When it comes to coaxing money out of the rich to help the poor, the Baroness is a Mayfair Mercenary of the highest order. This is not to say that like Peter York's blonde warriors of the eighties, sun-glasses on their heads and Gucci bags slung from the shoulder, she would never clamber into anything below the rank of a Porsche, but rather that she is a Charity Queen of renown.

Her principal work has been for UNICEF, UNESCO and the British Red Cross. Those more used to seeing her in a tiara, or as painted by Annigoni in a ballgown, might be surprised by her role on Sunday mornings, but she squeezes the Nescafé money from the Farm Street set with as much gusto as she gathers in charity donations from international bankers. Although proud of her English descent, she has spent much of her life in Florence, Paris and Monte Carlo. When she made her home in Mayfair nine years ago, a tweedy voice was heard asking at a reception, 'Who is this Baroness who has surged so suddenly into our midst?' Surging, it is generally agreed by those who love her, is a good word to describe Stefania. Whatever she takes on is done with boundless enthusiasm. She has a particular fond-ness for arranging parties on boats. If you see a launch full of beauties, bankers and foreign royalty floating down the Thames on a summer evening, and if it has aboard a string orchestra and Lord Archer, then ten to one the Baroness is holding a 'do' for a good cause.

Charity balls are part of the Mayfair way of life. Before the Second World War white tie and tails were *de rigueur*. The great hostesses lent their mansions freely for such parties, but after the War the hotels on Park Lane became fashionable on account of their enormous ballrooms. Devonshire House was famous for its philanthropy. In the aftermath of the French Revolution Duchess Georgiana gave a ball for 800 people to succour aristocrats fleeing from the Terror. Most had escaped by dressing in their servants' clothing and must have had a hard time finding costumes for such an assembly. Charles Dickens loved to use Devonshire House for his literary charities, which were keenly supported by Prince Albert. Victoria attended a benefit there for the Guild of Literature and Art in the year of the Great Exhibition. Dickens had written a sketch in which a character smoked a clay pipe, but as the Queen could not bear the smell of tobacco, the leading actor had to stride on stage amid wreaths of artificial smoke, created by attaching fine cotton wool to strands of quivering wire.

The novelist was a friend of Angela Burdett-Coutts, the multi-millionairess grandaughter of Thomas Coutts, the banker. Sometimes the good lady felt she had so much money that she didn't know the best means of giving it away. She lived in a modest house in Stratton Street, placing a Meissen cockatoo in her front window as a sign that she was in, or out. Depending on which way the cockatoo's beak faced her circle of close friends knew when to call. She took an active part in the management of the bank and loaned £50,000 to Princess Mary Adelaide, the spendthrift Duchess of Teck, who received only £2,000 a year from the Civil List and was a constant source of embarrassment to her cousin, the Queen. Known to the Londoners as 'Fat Mary' the Duchess was a popular figure, cheered loudly when she drove down Piccadilly in an open landau, but she could not control her purse strings. Each time she was rescued she over-spent again until Victoria and Albert despaired. They paid her debts, sternly warning her that it was 'for the last time' and banished the Tecks with their daughter the future Queen Mary, to Florence to economise. Mary Adelaide borrowed a splendid villa, courtesy of Coutts, and launched into a season of party-giving which doubled her expenditure.

As she grew older Angela Burdett-Coutts found philanthropy more rewarding than bank management. She regularly consulted Dickens, for the great writer was supposed to understand the needs of the poor better than they did themselves. The pair would meet at the Clarendon Hotel in Bond Street. In 1847 the fruit of their tête-à-têtes sent a frisson through Society. The heiress and the novelist founded Urania Cottage, a reformatory for prostitutes who wished to go straight. The women were taught practical skills to support themselves and then given assisted passages to Australia.

By roping in a celebrity of Dickens stature, Baroness Coutts set a high standard for future charity queens. In contemporary Mayfair fund raising events stick to a prescribed formula. A steering committee assembles. It flounders about a bit, then elects a Chairman with a track record for drawing in the cash. The Chairman should have a wide circle of friends, preferably including Pavarotti and Richard Branson. Pavarotti, who has a heart of gold, is so used to singing for his supper, that he was heard breathing sighs of relief recently at Highgrove when he was asked as a mere guest. After the chairman is chosen, a working committee settles down to decide on a venue, a date, the ticket prices and which night will suit Lord Archer. The novelist and Tory party supremo is London's most gifted auctioneer and on a busy night is whisked from function to function. As well as Lord Archer the committee sometimes decide at this point to have a logo to give the writing paper a distinctive appearance. Illustrations, however, can create drama. For last year's Midsummer Enchantment, in aid of the Red Cross, Andrew Lloyd Webber offered Baroness von Kories a fairy picture.

Lord Lloyd Webber, you understand, was not *giving* the picture to be auctioned by Lord Archer. It was just to be printed on the invitations – cards so elegant and so desirable that all London immediately coveted them. In full colour, and fiendishly expensive to re-print, they showed Oberon and Titania arguing and surrounded by a full complement of fairy courtiers in battle array. Huge quantities of invitations were printed and at every committee meeting the Baroness's helpers asked for more. Everyone, it seemed, wanted fairies on the mantlepiece, but ticket sales were not, at first, spectacular. The committee concluded people were enchanted by the picture, but that they were failing to look inside the card at details of the ball. It was then discovered that the evening chosen clashed with a World Cup semi-final.

Football fixtures are a particular nightmare for charity organisers. Chrysanthe Lemos, co-chairman of the Red Cross Winter Ball, was present when Placido Domingo was singing at Buckingham Palace in aid of one of Princess Diana's favourite charities, Birthright. Everyone was in evening dress listening to the Philharmonia Orchestra, while far away in a draughty stadium England played Germany. The first violinist was just working up to a passage of incredible sweetness, when a liveried footman came in with a folded piece of paper. He bowed silently and handed it to the Princess. Mr Lemos, the Greek ship-owner, was sitting immediately behind her. The Princess opened the paper, turned round and whispered, 'We lost.'

In the seventies and eighties Royalty was still the big draw at charity functions. Hundreds of people used to attend the Berkeley Square Ball in aid of the London hospitals, because when the marquee grew hot and the dancers spilled out under the plane trees, they stood a fair chance of having an *al fresco* chat with Princess Anne or Princess Margaret. Sadly the ball, which had become a popular fixture in the London Season was stopped because some residents complained of noise. 'All three residents,' as Sir Clive Sinclair, then Chairman of the Shepherd Market Association, remembers, which is fair comment, since RAM and ARM had been complaining that there hadn't been enough residents in Berkeley Square for decades.

As well as a working committee every self-respecting charity relies on an honorary committee, a list of 'names' chosen to lend weight and dignity to the event. I have always been considered good at producing Duchesses for such lists. It is a natural rather than an acquired talent, which silences PR ladies and leaves visiting Americans stunned. At the spectacular Shakespeare Globe Gala of 1990, I managed, unintentionally, to produce 'the Duchess who died'. She was Laura Marlborough, who lived in Portman Square, but was a consistent habituée of Mayfair and a staunch supporter of its favourite charity the Red Cross. During the War she lived at the Dorchester, but worked in the canteen – as 'a glorified barmaid' – at the Washington Hotel in Curzon Street where the American Forces were somewhat riotously billeted.

A distinguished raconteur, Laura wrote an autobiography, *Laughter from a Cloud*, which deserved to go into more editions. She said it would have, but that Lord Weidenfeld refused to reprint because it created such a stir when it came out that he feared libel actions. Née Charteris and successively Lady Long, Countess of Dudley, Mrs Michael Canfield and Duchess of Marlborough, Laura had lived an interesting life by anyone's standards. Her sister, Anne, married Ian Fleming, the creator of James Bond. During the Second World War, as Countess of Dudley, Laura turned Himley, her home in the Midlands, into a hospital for bomb-blasted servicemen, recovering from skin grafts. She was a friend of Sir Archibald McIndoe, the pioneer of plastic surgery. While the War was still in progress Laura married Eric Dudley and promptly organised one of the most remarkable fêtes the Red Cross has ever known. A hundred thousand people attended and the proceedings were opened by Mrs Churchill. Winston had promised to do the honours, but the Battle of Arnhem intervened. Laura followed up the Himley fête by riding for charity in a flat race on a horse called Firebrand. He won, but declined to stop at the winning post, circling the course for a further six rounds while a horrified Earl of Dudley screamed, 'Get my wife off that horse.'

Laura's Aunt Kakoo, the Duchess of Rutland, once sat on her, when as a baby she was placed by a nurse on her mother's bed. She was always accident prone, but this thought did not cross my mind when I asked her to support the then-unfinished Globe. Her name went on the writing paper and also on the stiff invitation cards. A few days later she called from the London Clinic. She had broken her arm. I took flowers and regaled her with Anglo–American committee stories for when glitterati of the two great nations get together in a good cause there are always opposing ideas on how things should be done. She laughed aloud and promised to be better for the gala. Many celebrities were to appear. It was the year Stephen Fry came into vogue and Ned Sherrin was producing the cabaret. The stiff invitations went out. Unfortunately, on the same morning they fell through the letter boxes, the better sort of papers carried Laura's obituary. I fancied I heard 'laughter from a cloud' but the Gala Chairman was distraught.

The Grosvenor House Hotel is a favourite venue for charity balls. Its special feature is the Great Room, which has two staircases leading from the gallery. It can hold 1,500 guests and is much sought after for extravaganzas and anything global. By London standards it has 'modern' air-conditioning, which was installed only ten years ago. For the Red Cross Winter Ball, Lord Archer had been booked well in advance and somebody had dreamed up the theme 'Spirit of Greece'. Naturally Mrs Lemos was called in as Chairman, but as she commutes between Athens, Montreux and Eaton Square, a co-chairman, Mrs Tina Chandris, had also been chosen. The committee were enthusiastic and one member, Pamela Jolyffe, who had lived twenty-seven years in Greece, happened to be a professional decorator. It did not seem possible for anything to go wrong and the World Cup was over. Peace, it was decided, should be the prevailing ethos. And what better for the decorations than a thousand olive branches?

Kenneth Turner, florist by royal appointment to that master-gardener HRH the Prince of Wales, promised to arrange them. With consummate professionalism Mrs Jolyffe came up with a design for the tables which delighted everyone. Tall vases of olive branches would decorate each table. Arranged round them in a cruciform shape would be low glass vases filled with water and olive oil, and floating in them little candelia, or wicks, which are lit as votive offerings in Greek churches. As the guests descended the twin staircases of the Great Room, they would look down on tiny pin-pricks of light and as they sat at the supper tables they would notice that the small glass vases held olive oil, the symbol of faith and eternity. A Greek jeweller offered brooches in the form of silver olive branches. Valentino gave bottles of scent. For the auction someone presented tickets for the next Olympic Games. There was also a Jaguar, a yacht and a safari holiday among the prizes.

The day of the ball dawned. Mrs Jolyffe and her team were at the hotel early. They had a mammoth task. An American committee member had donated specially blown glass containers in which the little wicks could float. Several thousand had been made in a Los Angeles glass factory and sent over by Federal Express. The ladies had to pull the wicks through them. In order that the olive oil would float decently upon the water, Mrs Jolyffe had enlisted her brother-in-law, a missiles expert of international repute, who headed a team of oil measurers. They worked efficiently and every vase contained precisely the same levels of water and oil. At the arranged hour Kenneth Turner's team of master-florists came to put the olive branches in the large vases. They fanned them out so gracefully that even the oil measurers paused to admire. Disaster did not strike until the florists had finished their work. The cabaret had just arrived for their technical rehearsal. The producer demanded that the lights be switched out so that he could test his own equipment. It was at this point that he noticed the olive branches. He screamed histrionically for them to be removed. The guests at the back, he argued, would not be able to see the show. In the end a compromise was reached and twenty vases were removed from the front tables, the very tables at which Mrs Lemos's guest of honour, ex-King Constantine of Greece, would sit.

The florists retired a trifle huffily. When they had gone the producer was still not satisfied. Arms flailing like a combine harvester, he went round the tables gathering the fanned branches into tall single columns, which allowed maximum vision. In the meantime Mrs Jolyffe's team had threaded the two thousandth wick through the two thousandth little glass bubble. Their fingers ached, but they were ready to finish their task. Unfortunately something had gone wrong at the Athenian wick-packing factory. The next layer of wicks – all 2,000 of them – were of the wrong thickness to thread through the remaining 2,000 little glass containers. The only solution was to take wicks from some vases and place them in others. By this time, however, the Grosvenor House staff had laid the tables. Silver and cloths showed each other off to gleaming perfection. The olive oil must not be allowed to drip. Mrs Jolyffe's nightmare continued to the eleventh hour, when the wick-lighting team set about igniting the tiny candelia. Those which lit looked beautiful – like little stars, but the air in a Greek Orthodox Church is still. The Grosvenor House air-conditioning was now blowing full blast to freshen the room for the expected throng. To Mrs Jolyffe and her wick lighters it felt like a Force 8 gale.

In the end the evening was a great success. The cabaret was superb, the food magnificent and the tiny candelia burned bright on their pools of olive oil. Only perfectionists could see that a few had apparently burned out, and a few not lit at all. Lord Archer raised a quarter of a million with the auction, chiding the bidders in his usual polite fashion,

'Come on, you mouldy things. What, only £65,000 for this lovely Jaguar? Come on, you mean shower. You can do better than that.' The international élite were a bit surprised, but they should know by now that the English take their pleasures sadly. Alas, for Mrs Jolyffe the evening was not done. After the ball was over the olive oil, so lovingly measured by the missiles expert had to be flushed away. The Grosvenor House staff flatly refused to have it poured down their drains and there was nothing for it, but to take the whole lot into Park Street and pour it down the Westminster Council's sewer. Questions were awaited with bated breath at the next meeting of the Mayfair Residents' Association from the team in charge of Waste and Refuse.

15
Flora and Fauna

There is no shortage of flora or fauna in Mayfair. It has three garden squares, a profusion of jasmine tumbling over brick walls, two private lawns, three top florists and a host of flower sellers. Peter of Bond Street is probably the most famous. Rain or shine he has sold ranunculus to duchesses for over thirty years under a striped awning between Asprey and Watches of Switzerland. Peter's clientéle is as grand as that of Ken Turner, who provides flowers for the horticulturally fastidious Prince of Wales. He remembers nostalgically the days when Marlene Dietrich wore violets, and his father pinned clove carnations into the buttonholes of 'real gents', who came out of the gaming clubs of St James's in the small hours. He remembers in particular one toff who always wore a cashmere coat back in the forgotten era when Sullivan and Powell still sold fine Turkish tobacco in the Burlington Arcade. Peter's father tucked the carnation in personally, so the young lord could continue to smoke in a relaxed and gentlemanly fashion, regardless of whether or not he had thrown away a fortune on the turn of a card. One day a puff of smoke became a raging conflagration, when the tip of the cigarette fell into the folds of the overcoat without either party noticing. The young lord did not come back. He only had one coat.

Of the top florists Mr Edward Goodyear, who builds arches of lilies around Claridge's doors, is the most distinguished. When Maureen, the late Marchioness of Dufferin and Ava held her ninetieth birthday party at Claridges, tiaras and white ties were worn. The floral tributes were banked so high around the hostess that the Star of Stars, not long recovered from a hip operation could not reach her to offer congratulations. Queen

One day a puff of smoke became a raging conflagration

Elizabeth, the Queen Mother, did not falter. She took to the floor with her equerry and calmly *waltzed* around the great wall of flowers. It takes a lot to fluster a former Empress of India.

Just as something in the air encourages people to buy flowers there, so something about Mayfair induces people to keep strange pets. Over the years the *Londoner's Diary* has specialised in W1 animal stories which go straight to the hearts of the British public. Take the time the crocodiles went missing from the Mayfair Hotel. Now the Mayfair Inter-Continental, the hotel went through a spectacular period in the sixties. It was owned by the Danziger Brothers, film producers who used special effects to create the Beachcomber, a Polynesian restaurant, where sunshine, clouds, and even thunder, alternated above a tiny lagoon. The two baby crocodiles were a star attraction, until the day they disappeared. Staff searched the building down to the last broom cupboard. Gagged and bound, the animals were eventually discovered on the steps of Savile Row Police Station. No one ever discovered the culprits. Students were suspected.

Mayfair is also the home of the Kennel Club, the HQ of British Dogdom, which has had premises in Clarges Street for over fifty years. The Kennel Club determines who enters Cruft's, the world's grandest dog show. Twenty thousand dogs go to Cruft's each year and with over a million pedigrees on its computers, the Kennel Club is surely the most class-conscious institution in the land. The first show was organised by Charles Cruft. It immediately attracted royal entrants. Queen Victoria showed her pet Pomeranians, Queen Alexandra was quick to follow with her magnificent Borzois. These aristocratic wolf hounds were given to Alexandra when she was Princess of Wales, by her cousin the Czar of Russia. In 1893 she exhibited 18 of them at Cruft's. She endeared herself to the nation by arriving to marry Prince Edward with two turtle doves, pets from her native Denmark. Word quickly got about that the new Princess was an animal lover, and she spent the rest of her life returning unsolicited gifts of fluffy puppies to the British public.

At Sandringham Alexandra kept a menagerie which included two Russian bears. Animals adored her. She bred and showed prize bantams and the celebrated Borzois were copied in town and country until they became the smart English gentlewoman's fashion accessory, as indispensable as the bustle. In 1904, when Alexandra had been Queen for a year, she spent £200 at a fair in aid of the Victoria Hospital for Children. Two Siamese cats, a terrier puppy, a pair of kids and a flying fox found their way to Buckingham Palace. The animals arrived before they were expected and were housed overnight in the Belgian Suite, usually reserved for foreign royalty. They escaped. Pandemonium ensued as they were rounded up by staff next morning, the flying fox clinging to a chandelier until he was dislodged by a footman with a broom handle. When Prince Edward finally proposed to the 17 year old Alexandra, the English Royal Family heaved sighs of relief and Queen Victoria gave her a sprig of white heather. The Prince had already gone through one amorous escapade with an actress called Nelly Clifden, and the Queen was convinced the shock had undermined Albert's health and hastened his premature death. She wished the marriage to take place as soon as possible and proposed 10 March. A horrified Archbishop of Canterbury pointed out that this date fell in Lent, to which the Queen replied, 'Marriage is a solemn duty and holy act *not* to be classed with amusements.' 'Darling Alix' was married in silver tissue and Honiton lace with eight bridesmaids in white crinolines, garlanded with pink roses. The Queen thought she would be 'soothing for Bertie'. Pink roses became associated with the Princess's charity work and in 1912, after King Edward's death, she founded the nation's first Flag Day, Alexandra Rose Day, which supports dozens of small voluntary charities. Alix cast a lasting spell over Mayfair with the Rose Ball, formerly at the Grosvenor House and now at the Inter-Continental Hotel, which traditionally begins the London Débutante Season.

The present Queen was born in Mayfair at 17, Bruton Street, the home of her parents, the Duke and Duchess of York. By 1935 the Yorks moved to 145, Piccadilly near Hyde Park Corner. Princess Elizabeth and Princess Margaret played with the children of their neighbour, Viscount Weymouth, later the sixth Marquis of Bath. The Weymouth children romped with their father's Welsh Corgi, Claire, and the two princesses begged their father, the future George VI, to buy one too. Jane and Dookie, the first royal Corgis, were delivered to 145, Piccadilly and photographed continuously with their new owners. Both princesses learned to swim in Mayfair at the Bath Club. In 1939 Princess Elizabeth got her life-saving certificate, provoking an outburst of sibling rivalry. Princess Margaret bundled Dookie into a lake and rushed in fully clothed after him. 'I saved him,' she announced proudly, cradling the startled animal against her dripping party frock. Dookie was immensely aristocratic. His half-brother was Champion Rozavel Red Dragon and after the Abdication he moved into Buckingham Palace.

For her 18th birthday Princess Elizabeth was given a Corgi called Susan, the ancestress of the present royal pack. As an owner-breeder the Queen conforms to Kennel Club rules. They have framed one of her registration forms at Clarges Street for Windsor Heather, a Corgi sired by the Queen Mother's Rozavel Beat the Band out of Rozavel Honey Bee. As a breeder the Queen has introduced a new strain the Dorgie, by crossing an ordinary Corgi with Princess Margaret's Dachshund, Pipkin. Susan is buried in the dog cemetery at Sandringham and Claire, who started it all, rests in peace at Longleat.

Exercising dogs can be a chore in Mayfair, as the traffic is so heavy. Small breeds, adept at flat-dwelling, are popular because they can easily be carried across roads. Sparkle, a champagne coloured Chihuahua, is a Mayfair Madam to the back teeth. She matches her mistress's fur coat and recently went to stay with London's most exclusive dog walker. This dog walker, you understand, is cousin to a fourteenth duke, so has an uncanny knack of noticing the finer eccentricities of animal behaviour. She spotted Sparkle limping in Hyde Park and discovered the Chihuahua had sore paws. She immediately rang the owner. 'Is your dog allergic to grass?' she asked. Sparkle's Mummy thought carefully 'I don't know', she replied. 'There isn't any grass in Mayfair.'

If you stand in the cosy executive quarters known as the Club on the twenty-sixth floor of the Park Lane Hilton and look down on W1 you will understand her dilemma. In Mayfair proper there is not a blade of grass to be seen. On the right is Green Park where early risers walk bull terriers and beyond it the soft outline of St James's Park, where Charles II used to exercise his spaniels. By craning your neck a little you can also see the green expanse of the Queen's back lawn, Corgi territory, rolling gently to the Buckingham Palace lake. Recently an urban fox hid there and ate some of Her Majesty's flamingoes. It was caught and deported to a rural environment.

None of these grasslands, however, fall strictly within the boundaries of Mayfair, which leaves the three great garden squares for dog walking, since private lawns, where they occur, are coveted for the erection of marquees. Since the banning of the Berkeley Square Ball, marquees are limited to the two lawns of note – the secret one behind Green Street where RAM holds its Summer Party and the glorious emerald patch in front of the Saudi Embassy in Curzon Street. Still known as Crewe House, after the Marquis who lived there, it was built by Edward Shepherd, when he had made his pile out of the Market. A long, low garden house, it has kept its rural ethos, so that the lawn is a veritable oasis in a desert of brick and stucco. A green and white striped marquee goes up for special occasions, such as Idl 'Fitr at the end of Rammadan or, at time of writing, the hundredth anniversary of King Ibn Saud capturing Riyadh after the desert tribes had been particularly revolting.

Now that Moyses Stevens has moved from Berkeley Square to Sloane Street, the Saudi lawn is one of the better places to find exotic flora. For Saudi National Day Mr Fuad Sebeih, who takes care of these matters, erected a luxuriously appointed marquee, entirely decorated with date palms. Mr Sebeih cherishes his lawn so lovingly that whenever a marquee goes up, special flooring is laid to protect the grass. The proceedings are watched with awe by the staff of Heywood Hill, the world-famous bookshop, where Nancy Mitford used to work. Dogs are not too highly rated in Saudi Arabia, except for Salukis, a princely breed used for hawking, but so far despite the present Ambassador's reputation as a distinguished poet, devoted to the spread of cultural values, no outbreaks of falconry have been reported in Curzon Street.

In the Green Street garden, a soft wisteria-filled place like a country manor, or courtyard, the dogs of certain well-heeled residents take exercise. Marquees have not previously been a worry, but a newly erected sundial may soon cause problems. It has been sited as a focal point of the very plot where the RAM Summer Party takes place (rumour has it that they will decamp to the Ritz). There are also three public areas, where well-behaved dogs may walk, but each has separate regulations. In the bleak savannahs of Grosvenor Square, stately green and gold waste bins proclaim the management of the Royal Parks with an attendant train of Serco gardeners, hedge clippers and bench minders. Benches are a big issue in Grosvenor Square. They have been nicked and even vandalised. Some say by tramps, others, more darkly, blame compulsive souvenir hunters attending farewell parties at the American Embassy. The usual dog rules apply however, 'Welcome on a lead'. In the sylvan reaches of Berkeley Square dogs on leads can walk sedately among the plane trees, but Westminster Council have put up a severe notice just opposite Annabel's front door, warning owners, 'Remember to use a scooper'. In Hanover Square, where schemes are afoot to change the planting from 'a few old roses' to seasonal beds, dogs on a lead are allowed, but pigeon feeding is forbidden. A ratio of ten litter bins to four dog waste units hints at priorities. Now that garden design has become such a national fetish, the Council means to replace all the metal litter bins with slatted wood – so rustic and deeply approved by English Heritage. In keeping too with the statue of Pitt the Younger and the awesome presence of Condé Nast, the parent company of *Tatler* and *Vogue*. *Tatler* has a particularly accusing piece recently, asking, 'Are you smart enough?'

At all corners of Hanover Square large pictures of birds with an obesity problem, daubed with a forbidding red cross, have been posted. I think this must be to assist foreign pigeons with language difficulties. The Royal Parks laugh Westminster to scorn on this score. 'You can't dictate where a pigeon flies', observed a maintenance executive meaningfully, but Westminster do have a bird nuisance on quite a different scale from anything experienced by the Royal Parks. Some myopic seagulls, excited by the great height of the residential buildings south of Oxford Street, have recently mistaken them for sea cliffs. They have taken to wheeling and dipping about the rooftops, emitting shrill screams, native to our shores, but unnerving to the urban population of the Peabody Trust, who dial 999 in the belief that ritual murder is being committed in Weighhouse Street.

To return to canine issues, the best place for a well-balanced dog to take exercise in Mayfair is undoubtedly Mount Street Gardens. This delightful enclave bounded by the Mayfair Library, Harry's Bar, the Grosvenor Chapel and Farm Street Church is adjacent to the Connaught Hotel, Scott's Restaurant, Allen's the butcher and the Audley Public House. It is thus the ideal spiritual, moral and gastronomic environment for the London dog and its owner. If a pious animal wants its Latin Mass, it can have it, but if it prefers a plainer form of worship, then the Rev Simon Hobbs is on hand at the Chapel, a very exclusive place of worship, which has Princess Margaret as Patron of the Restoration Appeal. The American Forces used the Grosvenor Chapel in the War to give thanks to God for the victory of the Allies. The Duke of Wellington's parents and Lady Mary Wortley Montague lie buried in the crypt. No one puts flowers there, which is sad. As one who did so much for our complexions, by introducing smallpox vaccination to these islands, Lady Mary deserves more veneration.

To get back to Mount Street Gardens, for a dog of breeding you can see the social and moral advantages straight away. He can get acquainted with a better class of Mayfair Madam for a start. No carbon monoxide fumes and the boles of some very nice plane trees for visiting. Dress is optional but the *Birmingham Post* once took pictures of Sir Henry Cotton's dogs, Trixie and Dolly, attired in black bows, when they attended the great golfer's funeral. Places were limited at Farm Street on that occasion, but knowing their master's last wishes, the exclusive dog-walker with the ducal relation booked seats for them in their full names of Lady Patricia and Lady Delissia Cotton. There was great excitement among the social columnists and sporting correspondents, as to who these female relations of the deceased might be. Lady Killearn's white poodle, the Hon Bubbles, has been spied in Mount Street Gardens, as has Digby the Shih-tzu. Of course there are a lot of amenities in the area to keep owners happy. Even in a quartier which boasts the Mirabelle, newly reincarnated by Marco Pierre White, and the timeless pleasures of Le Gavroche, Scotts, long famous for its oysters cannot be too highly praised. It is almost the last seafood restaurant in Central London to serve fish and chips with the proper traditional accompaniment of the mushy pea. Richoux do one round the corner in South Audley Street, but it is heavily minted.

Hard by at 117 Mount Street, Allen's, a really old-fashioned butcher of the calibre rarely found east of Somerset still uses huge wooden chopping tables and marble surrounds. When EU regulations outlawed sawdust, Allens must have been the last butcher's in London to dispense with the time-honoured floor covering. They have served top dogs in Mayfair from the present site for over 150 years, and before that had a shop where Purdey the gunsmith now stands. Like any first-class establishment Allen's *cannot* divulge the names of its regular customers, but some grand animals go there only for the best calves' liver and a number of Mayfair households still order specially minced filet for the dog's dinner. One canine gourmet touches nothing but free-range chickens, he rejects the battery fed kind at a sniff. Allen's do a nice line in chump chops, which have so far survived EU legislation, though I suppose it will only be a matter of time before lamb on the bone gets banned. If this happens, I am planning to get together with the Hon Bubbles, who has the advantage of a Harley Street address, to lobby for better NHS dental care for the carniverous classes. We hope to be photographed together in the top left-hand column of the *Londoner's Diary.* Bubbles is already sorting through his jewelled collars for the event.

16
Shopping to Impress

My mother was the grandest shopper I ever knew. I don't think she shopped consciously to impress, but whenever she went on a foray, she was followed by a train of assistants *carrying* things. A high sense of style had been bred into her by my grandmother, who lived in the South of France at that interesting period when the Russian aristocracy were milling about Monte Carlo, selling tiaras to survive. My grandmother adored *objets de vertu*. Her blouse buttons were by Fabergé and stray bits and pieces from the Ballets Russes kept finding their way into her wardrobe. When I read that the Russian Sale at Sotheby's – which included many of the Diaghilev costumes – brought in £5,000,000, I wished I hadn't given so many of grandmother's things to Oxfam. In London she shopped at Simpson's of Piccadilly in the days when it was an avant-garde thing to do. She was a snob about diamonds, fine china, Belgian chocolate, superior blends of tea and Beaune. A Russian Grand Duke once told her that Beaune was good for rheumatism and though a teetotaller in other respects she always bought some from Fortnum and Mason to guard against the twinges.

Grandmother had some nice jewellery. One of her friends was Mr Wartski of Llandudno, who acted as a sort of clearing house for Russian bric-à-brac, which found its way to North Wales. When I came to London as a young woman our family maxim was 'Asprey's for mending things and Wartski's if you should ever need to to sell'. At this point in my life parenthood was imminent and a lozenge of mother of pearl had fallen off the baby hairbrush. Unhesitatingly I took it to Asprey, who mended it for the sum of £2. This caused great offence to my mother-in-law, a connoisseur of Georgian silver, which she acquired with unerring thrift at country house sales and from obscure Welsh antique dealers. She considered Asprey an extravagance and renewed her efforts to teach me domestic economy by giving me a copy of *English Recipes Old and New*. It laid great emphasis on lentil soup and afternoon tea scones.

It was an alarmist gesture. I was not trying to impress by taking the baby hairbrush to Asprey. When a woman shops to impress she buys clothes. When a man shops to impress he buys a car, and if a man shops to impress a woman he drapes her in jewellery. It follows that quite a lot of spending to impress goes on in Mayfair. Not, of course among the indigenous English, who regard it as vulgar to show off. We natives tend to shop to please ourselves but English taste, so quietly understated, has become rather sought after, particularly now that Mayfair is a centre of world banking. A surprising horde of rich foreigners try to imitate us, so that a number of uniquely British institutions are facing a period of change. Take tea at the Ritz. Some years ago nothing was more soothing than to saunter into the foyer of the Ritz and have a nice cup of tea by the fountain, where goldfish browsed peacefully among the pondweed. One walked in by the revolving front door, which was on Piccadilly, and out by the Arlington Street entrance, all primed for a spot of shopping in St James's, or fortified to queue at the Royal Academy. Nowadays tea at the Ritz is so popular you have to book in advance. The front door is closed forever, and the chance of casually running into a friend who has popped in at the same moment has been halved.

Many English people are boycotting the Ritz as a protest against the closure of the front door, but the boycott is not fully effective as it was sabotaged when the Prince of Wales went to a party there with Mrs Parker Bowles and a train of attendant papparazzi. The hotel has suddenly become so busy that the management has not had time to notice the loss of its regular patrons. Many have decamped to Brown's Hotel in Albemarle Street, which is a safe haven of the English way of life and still serves plain scones for tea and turbot on the dinner menu. I miss the goldfish though. (Recent research shows that the two best therapies for high blood pressure are watching fish and stroking furry animals.) It is a pity His Royal Highness didn't go

Some years ago nothing was more soothing than to saunter into the foyer of the Ritz and have a nice cup of tea by the fountain . . .

partying at the Connaught. They give short shrift to papparazzi there. When the American President was staying some years ago, an aide from the White House telephoned and asked to be put through to Mr Nixon. 'Initial Sir?' said the switchboard operator. Now that's *real* discretion.

At the time of writing we are mourning the closure of another great British institution, Simpson's of Piccadilly. It was owned for years by Anthony Andrews's mother-in-law, Heddy Simpson. She was a *grande dame* of renown and knew how to order caviare with style. Bond Street too, once a byword for understated chic, is another bit of Mayfair succumbing to the winds of change. The stretch between Conduit Street and Cartier has suddenly become bright with banners announcing a high concentration of famous jewellers. Even Mr Clough the pawnbroker hangs out a green and yellow flag, while above Bentley & Skinner the Prince of Wales's feathers are picked out in cream and gold like something on a movie set. Asprey that erstwhile haven for mending things, was acquired by the Sultan of Brunei's brother, Prince Joffre, and later merged with Garrard, the Regent Street crown jewellers. A subtle change came over the window displays. At about the time of the merger, I went in with a friend who is a member of the polo playing classes. He stopped before a case filled with covetable earrings – little daisies encrusted with diamonds. Just for a moment my heart leaped. Was our twenty year friendship about to blossom into something deeper? After studying a tray of rings, my friend pointed to the largest in disgust and said, 'What decent Englishwoman would be seen with a thing like that on her hand?'

We Brits do self-restraint awfully well and as though to redress the balance, Asprey and Garrard set up a series of 'Shopping to Impress' windows, to reassure us that they are still inimitably English. Quotations were supplied by style gurus, who had been asked to select presents they would like to acquire for themselves. Mark Birley the proprietor of Annabel's longed for 'a fat decanter'. Jasper Conran coveted 'a perfect humidor for around a week's supply'. A designer cigar box in gleaming black wood mounted with silver knobs dominated his window. It was the size of a small chiffonier. In another window a herd of elephants, trunks waving, ears flapped back, indicated Lady Apsley's taste in ornamental silver. 'What a pleasure it would be to give or receive one of these beautiful pieces,' ran her quote. 'The grave intelligence and loyalty of the elephant has been a constant source of inspiration to me.' At £80,000 for the small size and £120,000 for the large, the beasts are rather a bargain. Round the corner in Grafton Street Wartski's have a tiny elephant in purpurine at £160,000. Purpurine is a *sang de boeuf* coloured glass, which was only made at the Imperial glass-works in St Petersburg. The art was lost after 1917.

In Grafton Street they favour a minimalist window display. Wartski do not *need* to advertise. Everyone likely to shop there knows that if you press the buzzer and are admitted through the small glass door, you will find yourself in the presence of a portrait of Queen Alexandra, bedizened with jewels. Around her neck are eleven ropes of pearls, the topmost mounted on silk to prevent chafing her skin. If you are a customer of repute, 'the Boss' Mr Kenneth Snowman, the world expert on Fabergé, will emerge from his office to greet you. That most acquisitive of royal collectors, Queen Mary, our present Queen's grand-mother, shopped at Wartski. They still keep her name on the writing paper beneath the royal appointments which are taste-fully embossed in crimson in lieu of a logo.

At Cartier they are even more laid back about advertising. Elephants are all the rage in Mayfair this season. A gold neck-lace of them walking trunk-to-tail can be gift-wrapped in the distinctive Cartier bag – red with gold lettering – but so many customers have had Rolex watches snatched that the Bond Street branch now keeps a supply of supermarket bags under the counter. The *dernier cri* is to leave the shop with half a million pounds' worth of pearls swathed in plastic and heavily disguised as shopping from Boots or Tesco. It is an old trick, of course. Before the War, when Claridge's flunkeys still wore red livery, Queen Alexandra of Yugoslavia, used to travel across Europe by train with the Crown Jewels in brown paper bags.

Cartier's reputation does rest on their diamonds. The most expensive diamond sold in modern times was the Star of the Season, which Sheik Ahmed Fitaihi bought from Sotheby's for $16.5 million. It ranks with the Koh-i-Noor, but the most *sensa-*

tional diamond acquired by Cartier was the pendant Richard Burton gave Elizabeth Taylor in 1969. Burton's agent was outbid at the Parke-Bernet sale in New York. This news was relayed to Richard and Elizabeth, who were in England dining at the Bell in Aston Clinton. Burton bought the 69.42 carat stone from Cartier and was taken to task for vulgarity by the *New York Times*. Elizabeth spent a further £40,000 on a diamond necklace from which the jewel could be hung. Lloyds specified in the insurance policy that it had to be kept in a vault and that an armed guard must be in attendance whenever Elizabeth wore it. The actress, who had been a star since her teenage debut in *National Velvet*, developed a surefire line in ripostes. When Princess Margaret told Elizabeth she thought that another of her trophies, the Krupp diamond, was the most vulgar piece she had ever seen, Elizabeth slipped the flashing jewel off her own finger and placed it on PM's. 'There now it doesn't look so vulgar,' she said sweetly.

We thespians tend to be impressive drinkers, and you can now pay almost as much for a bottle of wine in Mayfair, as for a good diamond. £105,000 is the top recorded price. The American actor Johnny Depp, in London to film *Sleepy Hollow*, recently spent £11,000 on a bottle of Burgundy at the Mirabelle, when he took his French girlfriend there. Poor Johnny Depp, perhaps he wasn't spending to impress, but the wine went straight to his head, for he hit a photographer after drinking it. I don't know why the Screen Actor's Guild doesn't take more care of its performers. You wouldn't get us Equity members falling into a trap like that. It was a bottle of Romané Conti 1978, and if Johnny had settled for an evening at home, he could have bought the '61 vintage of the same wine for two and a half thousand pounds down the road at Fortnum & Mason. It isn't quite up to the standard of the '78, but for anyone feeling tired and emotional after a hard day's filming, it might have been a better bet. Not, of course, that I wish to knock the Mirabelle's corkage charge. I don't want that Marco Pierre White banning me from crossing his thresholds. 'On paie l'ambience' as the French would say and down at Le Meridien in Piccadilly, where the great chef presides over the Oak Room, the vinaigrette of leeks and langoustines with *caviare en gelée* is to die for.

I am not a great wine snob myself. Berry Bros., the oldest wine shop in St James's, take care of my modest needs. Berry's were founded in 1698, nine years before Fortnum & Mason. Their selections are impeccable and their credit elastic. If one forgets to pay an account they send a most courteous reminder on cream writing paper. If anyone wanted to give me a birthday surprise, I would hint that a Chateau Cheval Blanc '85 would do nicely. Berry's are getting very coy about these matters. They print 'Prices on request' in the current list, but Fortnum's do a Cheval Blanc '82, which is a bargain at £525 – the bottle of course, not the case. It is a far cry from the Beaunes, recommended by Grandma's Grand Duke. Nowadays they seem on a par with your average Chasse Spleen. Perhaps the palate is getting jaded and I am not allowing for the appreciation which accrues from laying down fine wines. Caviare prices, though, can put me in a fine passion. An establishment has opened in Mayfair which prides itself on supplying corporate gifts. It lists Beluga, Oscietre, and Sevruga among them. Such pretensions! Corporate caviare indeed. It's a contradiction in terms.

The approved place to eat caviare in Mayfair is Kaspia, the restaurant in Bruton Place with the duck egg blue table cloths and a picture of Tsar Nicholas I behind the bar. Kaspia started up in Paris in 1927. The London branch was a natural offshoot. When it first opened, Lady Bayliss, the proprietor's mother, made the chocolate cakes. One wit reckoned that lessened the gap between trade and Society, but the chief glory is the vodka selection – thirty different varieties running from the Bison Grass favoured by Russian huntsmen to the Smirnoff Black Label filtered through Siberian silver birch charcoal, according to the old Imperial method. There is no hype on the menu. Blinis can be eaten with affordable pressed caviare. Krug is not the house champagne, but it is in plentiful supply and a few customers still order Beluga the traditional way – by the bucketful. It makes the 'glass caviar server with silver rim' recommended for corporate gift giving by 'the other place' seem a trifle stingy.

Bruton Place is the last sanctuary for anyone not shopping to impress, but with the spending power to do so. At Melton's, the interior decorators who specialise in 'style anglaise', Digby the

117

Shih-tzu snoozes among the chintzes. Further down the street the *Turf* newspaper, bible of British racegoers, has its HQ and the revered Sladmore Gallery still sells special editions of bronze animal sculptures by Rembrandt Bugatti, the talented brother of the racing car designer, Ettore, who died so tragically at 31. A wild boar scowls magnificently from the window and a Carlo Bugatti chair (not for sale) looks as though it might have come fresh from an Egyptian tomb. Across the street Holland and Holland, the gunsmiths have a window to their ladies' department. They sell beautifully cut country clothes in colours that won't frighten the horses, but will still leave the International Set drooling with envy. This season's corn coloured shooting jacket with a tiny hint of mustard seed is a case in point. Hot colours for bikinis and party shoes we should leave to the Italians, but soft shades for the point-to-point or the country house weekend is a field in which we Brits excel.

Shoe shopping is still best done in Bond Street, where Gucci, Ferragamo and Russell & Bromley vie to outdo each other. F. Pinet on the corner of Maddox Street and Bond Street have been there for over sixty years. They are now owned by Russell & Bromley, who have wisely not interfered with the décor, for to sit in Pinet on the grey velvet sofas trying on an evening sandal studded with rhinestones is to feel like a fairy princess. It may explain why some addicts need to visit a therapist. Shoeaholics sometimes have to be cured by visits to a hypnotist. The disease is not just confined to Imelda Marcos. Supermodels and ex-models get peculiarly addicted. One Bond Street shopper who had given up her modelling career for the tranquillity of a good marriage, was recently delighted to be asked back to 'do a little PR' for a leading shoe store. As soon as the cameras began to click, she was off. They surrounded her with a hundred pairs of shoes, and the photographer soon had her tossing them in the air and catching them with laughter in her eyes. The feature appeared in a Sunday newspaper. The Senior Partner of her husband's bank rang up and said sympathetically, 'No wonder you need a further overdraft. Your wife is *very* pretty, but she does seem to buy a lot of shoes.'

The incident left the lady near to tears. She went to Valentino and put £8,000 worth of clothing on her account in compensation. By that time most of her husband's elderly relatives were writing him letters of condolence, filled with quotations from the *Talmud* about the duties of a virtuous wife. She didn't know which way to turn and asked Valentino to let her return the unworn outfits. To her eternal surprise, they did.

Colour matched cars are another common fashion accessory among the super rich. Jack Barclay in Berkeley Square, purveyors of Rolls-Royces to anyone who can afford true craftsmanship is another institution which has retained its native charm, despite the injection of a little foreign capital. VW have wisely decided not to change the showroom or the staff. Stories abound about other people's shopping habits, although of course the staff are the soul of discretion and would never divulge names. Peter Pitt-Brown remembers a lady in the 1980s who bought five cars in eight weeks. She came in for a Rolls-Royce Silver Spirit, paid for it and reappeared a week later. 'Mr Pitt Brown, I'd like to buy another.' Two weeks later the purchaser returned. 'I'd like two more please, in different colours'. Jack Barclay's staff are very discreet and they never ask why, but at the fourth visit, Mr Pitt-Brown's curiosity overcame him and he ventured to ask why the lady needed so many motor cars.

'Oh, they're all presents.'

Two months later the lady appeared again. First names were used this time. 'Hello, Peter, I need another one.' In 1980 the going price for a Silver Spirit was £48,000 and in those days that was a considerable sum.

Another lady customer came in with a well-known surgeon. She asked him if he liked a beige Silver Shadow which was standing in the showroom. He did. Some days later the lady returned in a state of great excitement, announcing she would buy it. She produced the money in notes from a plastic bag and asked for the car to be delivered to the hospital where the surgeon worked, with a big bunch of flowers on the back seat. 'Don't tell anyone. It's a surprise.' The Rolls was duly delivered to the hospital, with flowers from Moyses Stevens and the keys in an envelope. Three days afterwards the surgeon walked into Jack Barclay and greeted Mr Pitt-Brown. He explained that he had gone to his work and 'There was a car there'. He looked Mr Pitt-Brown in the eye, 'Did you have anything to do with it?'

119

'Well, I can't tell you who sent it, but as a matter of fact, I did. Is it all right, sir? There isn't anything wrong?'

'I don't like the colour.' A deep metallic green was substituted for the offending beige.

A modern Silver Seraph would cost around £155,000 – roughly the same as a Fabergé elephant. Any amount of modifications can be made because the team at the Rolls-Bentley factory in Crewe and the staff at Berkeley Square like the finished model to 'reflect the wishes of the customer'. There is no design team as such. They have been asked to match a Silver Spirit Estate to a lady's lipstick, they have had a customer send in a jug and a flowered scarf as colour guides for a particular finish. They can offer the very latest in satellite navigation, and cars fitted with TV screens, faxes and fridges. They are asked for accessories like vanity mirrors which retract into the ceiling and their clients come from all walks of life – bookmakers and actors receive the same courteous deference as heads of state. They are not innovators at Jack Barclay, they are perfectionists. Should anyone be vulgar enough to enquire which car is most likely to impress, they have the perfect answer – a Rolls-Royce is a statement; a Bentley is an understatement.